Praise for

SHORT BIKE RIDES IN RHODE ISLAND

"Awaken the adventure in yourself by using **Short Bike Rides in Rhode Island** to plan out a bicycle route that will let you truly discover Rhode Island ... Stone's delightful dialogue makes this an easy reader. Stone's thorough descriptions include historical glimpses of the state."
    —The *Rhode Island Herald*

"Each [of his bike books] involves hours of research using topographic maps and countless hours of road-testing each ride 'mainly for safety and pleasantness.' "
    The *Sunday Journal* (RI) *Magazine*

"... Wonderfully illustrated with black and white photographs and sample routes."
    —The *Library Journal*

"If you're a bicyclist and fully want to enjoy the colorful change of the seasons, I strongly recommend taking a copy of **Short Bike Rides in Rhode Island** with you."
    —*Rhode Island Woman* magazine

"... Keeps you organized and informed as you pedal through the back roads."
    —*Women's Sports and Fitness* magazine

SHORT BIKE RIDES IN RHODE ISLAND

Third Edition

by Howard Stone

An East Woods Book

The Globe Pequot Press

Chester, Connecticut

Library of Congress Cataloging-in-Publication Data

Stone, Howard, 1947-
    Short bike rides in Rhode Island.
    1. Bicycle touring—Rhode Island—Guide-books.
2. Rhode Island— Description and travel—1981-
—Guide-books. I. Title.
GV1045.5.R4S8 1988   917.45   88-6119
ISBN 0-87106-721-8

Manufactured in the United States of America
Third Edition/First Printing

To the memory
of Warren Hinterland,
who inspired me

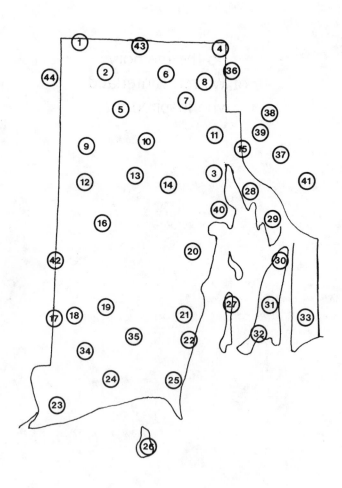

Table of Contents

Preface to the Third Edition

The third edition of *Short Bike Rides in Rhode Island* follows the same format as the second edition, with an introductory description, map, and point-to-point directions for each ride. The rides are essentially the same, but the maps and directions have been updated for accuracy and clarity. In about half the rides I have changed the route slightly to take advantage of better roads or to improve safety and scenery. I have added one new ride, an 18-mile loop starting from North Scituate.

The major changes are as follows: On the Warwick rides, I have deleted two small peninsulas, which are now strictly private. I have lengthened the Cumberland–Wrentham–Plainville ride by a few miles to include the fine scenery along West Wrentham Road, which has recently been repaved. I also added a new ten-mile shortcut to this popular ride. On Ray Young's Ride, newly-paved Cranberry Ridge Road and Paris Iron Road were substituted (with Ray's approval, of course) for the bumpier Huntinghouse Road and Snake Hill Road. On the Hope Valley–North Stonington ride, a deteriorating section of Route 3 has been rerouted onto back roads. On the East Greenwich–North Kingstown ride, I have substituted South Road for the bumpier Stony Lane. The Wakefield rides now start at the new Salt Pond Shopping Center, which is on a safer road. The Barrington ride now follows the newly constructed East Bay Bike Path, which is a delight to bicycle along. All three Seekonk–Rehoboth rides now go through lovely Rehoboth Village.

I would like to thank Sandra Gallup, my supervisor, for allowing me to work flexible hours so that I could take advantage of the daylight to go over the rides. I would also like to thank John Darcy for helping me verify some of the routes.

Introduction

Bicycling is an ideal way to appreciate the New England landscape's unique intimacy, which is not found in most other parts of the United States. The back roads turn constantly as they hug the minute contours of the land, forcing your orientation down to a small scale. Every turn and dip in the road may yield a surprise—a weathered barn, a pond, a stream, a little dam or falls, a hulking old Victorian mill right out of the Industrial Revolution, a stone wall or a pasture with grazing cattle or horses. Many of the smaller town centers are architectural gems, with the traditional stately white church and village green flanked by graceful old wooden homes and the town hall.

Rhode Island, along with the sections of Massachusetts and Connecticut adjoining the state line, offers ideal cycling. The area is blessed with an impressive network of hundreds of back roads, most of them paved but not heavily travelled. Beyond the Providence metropolitan area the landscape is rural enough to give the cyclist a sense of remoteness and serenity, and yet the nearest town, village, or grocery store is never more than a few miles away. The terrain is refreshingly varied for such a small area.

The eastern border or Rhode Island, and nearby Massachusetts, contains flat and gently rolling farm land, with some large areas of cleared land. The western and northern sections of the state consist primarily of wooded, hilly ridge-and-valley country dotted with ponds, small farms, and mill villages. To the south are some of the finest beaches on the East Coast and the beautiful, largely unspoiled shoreline of Narragansett Bay.

The Geography of the Region

Rhode Island is shaped roughly like a triangle with the top chopped off, measuring about 20 miles along the northern border, 35 miles along the southern shore, and 45 miles from north to south along the Connecticut border. Narragansett Bay, Rhode Island's most prominent and scenic natural feature, extends two-thirds of the way up into the state and splits it into two unequal sections, with the segment east of the bay a slendor Filament only two to five miles wide. The bay itself contains three large islands and several small ones.

In general, the land east of Narragansett Bay extending into Massachusetts is flat, and everything else is rolling or hilly except for a narrow coastal strip. As a result, biking in Rhode Island involves some effort. Most of the rides contain at least one or two hills, sometimes steep or long enough so that you'll want to walk them. To compensate, however, there are no hills that are long enough to be really discouraging, and for every uphill climb there's a corresponding downhill run. The large majority of the hills you'll encounter are under a half mile long, with the steepest portion being limited to a couple hundred yards or less.

Culturally, Rhode Island is a product of the long and varied history that has nurtured New England. The deep and sheltered waters of Narragansett Bay, which spawned thriving seaports and maritime commerce in colonial times, is now one of the boating capitals of America. The splendid coastline prompted the growth of gracious beachfront communities for the affluent, such as Watch Hill, Narragansett Pier, and the most famous of all, Newport. The Industrial Revolution began in America in 1793 with the Slater Mill in Pawtucket. In later years, culminating in the period between the end of the Civil War and the turn of the century, hundreds more mills were built along the swift-flowing Blackstone, Pawtuxet, Pawcatuck and other rivers, manned by waves of immigrants from Europe and French Canada.

Today Rhode Island's many mill villages comprise one of the state's most appealing and architecturally fascinating hallmarks. Typically, a mill village contains one or two grim red-brick granite mills, foreboding but ornamented with cornices and clock towers, and flanked by an orderly row of identical two- or three-story houses, originally built for the workers during the late 1800s. Adjacent to the mill is a small pond with a little dam or falls. Unfortunately, fire, neglect, and vandalism claim several mills each year, but a growing consciousness has arisen toward preserving and maintaining these unique and impressive buildings. Many old mills have been recycled into apartments or condominiums.

Conditions for bicycling at the state level have made great progress in the last few years. The most noteworthy accomplishment is the completion of a four-mile section of the East Bay Bicycle Path between Riverside Square in East Providence and the center of Barrington. The path is well–designed and constructed, heavily used, and a delight to ride. Eventually it will run about fifteen miles from the Washington Bridge (Route 195) in Providence to Independence Park in Bristol. A more ambitious project, now in the planning stage, is a 19-mile bikeway along the Blacktone River from the Washington Bridge to Blacktone, Massachusetts. The bikeway, which will run partly on bicycle paths and partly on existing roads, is to be a portion of a linear historical park along the river. Finally, many state roads (most notably Routes 102, 91, 108, and 2) have been or are being resurfaced and widened with good shoulders.

About the Rides

Ideally a bicycle ride should be a safe, scenic, relaxing, and enjoyable experience that brings you into intimate contact with the landscape. In striving to achieve this goal, I've routed the rides along paved secondary and rural roads, avoiding main highways, cities, and dirt roads as much as possible. I've tried to make the routes as safe as possible. Hazardous situations such as very bumpy roads or dead stops coming down a steep hill have been avoided except for a few instances with no reasonable alternate route. Any dangerous spot has been clearly indicated in the directions by a **Caution** warning. I've included scenic spots like dams, falls, ponds, mill villages, ocean views, or open vistas on the rides wherever possible.

Nearly all the rides have two options—a shorter one averaging about 15 miles, and a longer one that is usually between 25 to 30 miles. All the longer rides are extensions of the shorter ones, with both options starting in the same way. A few rides have no shorter option. All the rides make a loop or figure eight rather than going out and then backtracking along the same route. For each ride I include a map and directions.

If you've never ridden any distance, the thought of riding 15, or, heaven forbid, 30 miles may sound intimidating or even impossible. I want to emphasize, however, that *anyone* in normal health can ride 30 miles and enjoy it if you get into a bit of shape first, which you can accomplish painlessly by riding at a leisurely pace for an hour several times a week for two or three weeks. If you bought this book and aren't bedridden, you can go out and bike 15 miles right now—guaranteed! If you're already engaged in a physical activity like tennis, racquetball, swimming, or jogging a couple of times a week, or have a job in which you're walking around or lifting things all day, you can hop on your bike and ride 30 miles right now—guaranteed! You've probably gone on a two-or three-hour ride at some time or other—if so, chances are you rode 15 or 20 miles without even realizing it. If you think of the rides by the hour rather than the mile, the numbers are much less frightening. Then you can tell your sedentary, chain-smoking friends that you biked 25 miles and watch their mouths drop open with astonishment and admiration.

To emphasize how easy bicycle riding is, most bike clubs have a hundred-mile ride, called a Century, each fall. Dozens of ordinary people try their first Century without ever having done much biking, and finish it, and enjoy it! Sure they're tired at the end, but they've accomplished the feat and loved it. (If you'd like to try one, the Narragansett Bay Wheelmen host the biggest and flattest Century in the Northeast on the Sunday after Labor Day, starting from Tiverton—ask at any bike shop or contact the Narragansett Bay Wheelman, Box 1317, Providence, RI 02901 for details.)

Not counting long stops, a 15-mile ride should take about two hours at a leisurely speed, a 20- to 25-mile ride about three hours, and a 30-mile ride about four hours. If you ride at a brisk pace, subtract an hour from these estimates.

I have intentionally not listed the hours and fees of historic sites because they are subject to so much change, often from one year to the next. If it's a place you've heard of, it's probably open from 10 a.m. to 5 p.m., seven days a week. Unfortunately, many of the less frequently visited spots have limited hours—often only weekday afternoons during the summer, perhaps one day during the weekend. A few places of historic or architectural interest, like the Eleazar Arnold House in Lincoln, are open only by appointment. The reason is a matter of funding and manpower. Most historic sites are maintained only by voluntary contributions and effort, and it's simply impossible to keep them staffed more than a few hours a day or a few months a year. If you really want to visit a site, call beforehand to find out the hours.

About the Maps

The maps are reasonably accurate, but I have not attempted to draw them strictly to scale. Congested areas may be enlarged in relation to the rest of the map for the sake of legibility. All the maps contain these conventions:

1. The maps are oriented with North at the top.
2. Route numbers are circled.
3. Small arrows alongside the route indicate direction of travel.
4. The longer ride is marked by a heavy line. The shorter ride is marked by a dotted line where the route differs from that of the longer ride.
5. I've tried to show the angle of forks and intersections as accurately as possible.

Enjoying the Rides

You will enjoy biking more if you add a few basic accessories to your bike and bring a few items with you.

1. Handlebar bag with transparent map pocket on top. It's always helpful to have some carrying capacity on your bike. Most handlebar bags are large enough to hold tools, a lunch, or even a light jacket. If you have a map or directions in your map pocket, it's much easier to follow the route. You simply glance down to your handlebar bag instead of fishing map or directions out of your pocket and stopping to read them safely. You may also wish to get a small saddlebag that fits under your seat, or a metal rack that fits above the rear wheel, to carry whatever doesn't fit in the handlebar bag.

Always carry things on your bike, not on your back. A knapsack raises your center of gravity and makes you more unstable; it also digs painfully into your shoulders if you have more than a couple of pounds in it. It may do for a quick trip to the grocery store or campus, but never for an enjoyable ride where you'll be on the bike for more than a few minutes.

2. Water bottle. It's nice to be able to take a drink whenever you wish, especially in hot weather. On any ride of more than 15 miles, and any time the temperature is above 80 degrees, you will get thirsty, and it's important to have water with you. On longer rides through remote areas, you should bring more than one full water bottle.

3. Basic tools. Always carry a few basic tools with you when you go out for a ride, just in case you get a flat or a loose derailleur cable. Tire irons, a six-inch adjustable wrench, a small pair of pliers, a small standard screwdriver, and a small Phillips-head screwdriver are all you need to take care of virtually all roadside emergencies. A rag and a tube of hand cleaner come in handy if you have to handle your chain. If your bike has any Allen nuts (nuts with a small hexagonal socket on top), carry metric Allen wrenches to fit them. Cannondale makes a handy one-piece kit with four Allen wrenches, along with a standard and Phillips-head screwdriver.

4. Pump and spare tube. If you get a flat, you're immobilized unless you can pump up a new tube or patch the old one. Installing a brand new tube is less painful than trying to patch the old one on the road. Do the patching at home. Pump up the tire until it's hard, and you are on your way. Carry the spare tube in your handlebar bag, or wind it around the seat post, but make sure it doesn't rub against the rear tire.

If you bike a lot, you'll get flats—it's a fact of life. Most flats are on the rear wheel, because that's where most of your weight is. You should therefore practice taking the rear wheel off and putting it back on the bike, and taking the tire off and putting it on the rim, until you can do it confidently. It's much easier to practice at home than to fumble at it by the roadside.

5. Dog repellent. When you ride in rural areas you're going to encounter dogs, no two ways about it. Even if you don't have to use it, you'll have peace of mind, knowing you have something like ammonia or commercial dog spray to repel an attacking dog if you have to. More on this later.

6. Bicycle computer or odometer. A bicycle computer or odometer provides a much more reliable way of following a route than depending on street signs or landmarks. Street signs are often nonexistent in rural areas or are rotated 90 degrees by mischievous kids. Landmarks such as "turn right at green house" or "turn left at Ted's Market" lose effectiveness when the green house is repainted red or Ted's Market goes out of business. A computer is much easier to read than the traditional odometer, because it sits on top of your stem and has large, clear digits. Most computers indicate not only distance, but also speed, elapsed time, and cadence. The solarpowered models last a long time before the batteries need replacement.

7. Bike lock. This is a necessity if you're going to leave your bike unattended. The best locks are the rigid, boltcutter-proof ones like Kryptonite and Citadel. The next best choice is a strong chain or cable that can't be quickly severed by a normal-sized boltcutter or hacksaw. A cheap, flimsy chain can be cut in a few seconds, and is not much better than no lock at all.

In urban or heavily touristed areas, always lock both wheels as well as the frame to a solid object, and take your accessories with you when you leave the bicycle. Many a cyclist ignoring this simple precaution has returned to the vehicle only to find one or both wheels gone, along with the pump, water bottle, and carrying bags.

8. Rear-view mirror. A marvelous safety device, available at any bike shop, which enables you to check the situation behind you without turning your head. Once you start using a mirror you'll feel defenseless without it. Mirrors are available to fit on eyeglasses, a bike helmet, or the handlebars. If you don't wear glasses, buy a cheap pair of sunglasses and remove the lenses.

9. Bike helmet. Accidents happen, and a helmet will protect your head if you fall or crash. Bike helmets are light and comfortable, and more and more cyclists are using them.

10. Food. Always bring some food with you when you go for a ride. It's surprising how quickly you get hungry when biking. Some of the rides go through remote areas with no food along the way, and that country store you were counting on may be closed on weekends or out of business. Fruit is nourishing and includes a lot of water. A couple of candy bars will provide a burst of energy for the last ten miles if you are getting tired. (Don't eat candy or sweets before then—the energy burst lasts only about an hour, they your blood-sugar level drops to below where it was before and you'll be really weak.)

11. Bicycling gloves. Gloves designed for biking, with padded palms and no fingers, will cushion your hands and protect them if you fall. For maximum comfort, use foam-rubber handlebar padding also.

12. Bike rack. It is much easier to use a bike rack than to wrestle your bike into and out of your car or trunk. Racks that attach to the back of the car are most convenient—do you really want to hoist your bike over your head onto the roof? If you use a rack that fits onto the back of the car, make sure that the bike is at least a foot off the ground and that the bicycle tire is well above the tailpipe. Hot exhaust blows out tires!

13. Light. Bring a bicycle light and reflective legbands with you in case you are caught in the dark. Ankle lights are lightweight, and bob up and down as you pedal for additional visibility.

14. Roll of electrical tape. You never know when you'll need it.

Before you begin riding, adjust your seat to the proper height and make sure it is level. I'm always amazed at how many cyclists have their seat much too high or low, or have it tilted either up or down. If your seat is at the improper height, you'll be uncomfortable, lose power and leverage when pedaling, and put needless strain on your knees and ligaments. It's best to adjust the seat with a friend who can hold the bike firmly while you mount it in riding position with the pedal arms vertical. When your seat is at the proper height, the knee of your extended leg should be slightly bent when you place the balls of both feet directly over the pedal spindles (the proper placement while riding). Then put both heels on the pedals. Your extended leg should now be straight, and you should be able to backpedal without rocking your fanny from side to side. If it rocks, the seat is too high; if your leg is still bent with the pedal arms at six and twelve o'clock, the seat is too low.

It's easiest to check whether your seat is level by placing a long board or broom handle on top of it lengthwise. Also check that the seat is not too far forward or back. When the pedal arms are horizontal, your forward knee should be directly over the pedal spindle. Again, a friend is helpful when you make the adjustments.

Take advantage of your gearing when you ride. It's surprising how many people with ten- or twelve-speed bikes use only two or three of their gears. It takes less effort to spin your legs quickly in the low or middle gears than to grind along in your higher ones. For leisurely biking, a rate of 60 to 70 revolutions per minute, or slightly more than one per second, is comfortable. If you find yourself grinding along at 40 or 50 RPMs, shift into a lower gear. Time your RPMs periodically on a watch with a second hand or your bicycle computer—keeping your cadence up is the best habit you can acquire for efficient cycling. You'll be less tired at the end of a ride, and avoid strain on your knees, if you use the right gears.

You will find it much easier to climb hills if you get a freewheel (the rear cluster of gears) that goes up to 34 teeth instead of the standard 28 teeth. You may also have to buy a new rear derailleur to accommodate the larger shifts, but the expense will be more than worthwhile in ease of pedaling. You can obtain even lower gears by putting a smaller chainwheel in the front, or converting your bike to a fifteen-speed. This alteration is quite expensive and not necessary for leisurely riding.

When approaching a hill, always shift into low gear *before* the hill, not after you start climbing it. If it's a steep or long hill, get into your lowest gear right away and go slow to reduce the effort. Don't be afraid to walk up a really tough hill; it's not a contest, and you're out to enjoy yourself.

Pedal with the balls of your feet, over the spindles, not your arches or heels. Toe clips are ideal for keeping your feet in the proper position on the pedals; they also give you added leverage when going uphill. The straps should be *loose* so that you can take your feet off the pedals effortlessly.

Eat before you get hungry, drink before you get thirsty, and rest before you get tired. To keep your pants out of your chain, tuck them inside your socks. Wear pants that are as seamless as possible. Jeans or cut-offs are the worst offenders; their thick seams are uncomfortable. Use a firm, good-quality seat. A soft, mushy seat may feel inviting, but as soon as you sit on it the padding compresses to zero under your weight, so that you're really sitting on a harsh metal shell.

Using the Maps and Directions

Unfortunately, a book format does not lend itself to quick and easy consultation while you're on your bike. The rides will go more smoothly if you don't have to dismount at each intersection to consult the map or directions. You can solve this problem by making a machine copy of the directions and carrying it in your map pocket, dismounting occasionally to turn the sheet over or to switch sheets. Most people find it easier to follow the directions than the map.

In the directions, I have indicated the name of a road if there was a street sign at the time I researched the route, and I did not indicate the name of the road if the street sign was absent. Street signs have a short life span—a couple of years of the average—and are often nonexistent in rural areas. Very frequently, the name of a road changes without warning at a town line, crossroads, or other intersection.

Using a bicycle computer or odometer is virtually essential to enjoy the rides. The directions indicate the distance to the next turn or major intersection. Because so many of the roads are unmarked, you'll have to keep track accurately of the distance from one turn to the next. It is helpful to keep in mind that a tenth of a mile is 176 yards, or nearly twice the length of a football field.

In writing the directions, it is obviously not practical to mention every single intersection. Always stay on the main road unless directed otherwise.

In the directions, certain words occur frequently, and so let me define them to avoid any confusion.

To "bear" means to turn diagonally, at an angle between a right-angle turn and going straight ahead. In these illustrations, you bear from road A onto road B.

To "merge" means to come into a road diagonally, or even head-on, if a side road comes into a main road. In the examples, road A merges into road B.

A "sharp" turn is any turn sharper than 90 degrees; in other words, a hairpin turn or something approaching it. In the examples, it is a sharp turn from road A onto road B.

Each ride contains a few introductory paragraphs that mention points of interest along the route or sometimes a short distance off it. Usually I do not mention these places again in the directions themselves, to keep them concise. If you'd like to keep aware of points of interest while doing the ride, make a note of them first, so you won't have to flip back and forth between the directions and the introduction. It is a good idea to read over the entire tour before taking it, in order to familiarize yourself with the terrain, points of interest, and places requiring caution.

Many riders have asked why books of bike rides aren't published in loose-leaf form, with map-pocket-sized pages. The answer comes down to economics—any format other than the standard paperback would double the price of the book unless the press run were enormous. Also, a loose-leaf book would require a special binding or portfolio, which would make the item clumsier to display in bookstores.

Safety

It is an unfortunate fact that thousands of bicycle accidents occur each year, with many fatalities. Almost all cycling accidents, however, are needless and preventable. Most accidents involve children under sixteen, and are caused by foolhardy riding and failure to exercise common sense. The chances of having an accident can be reduced virtually to zero by having your bike in good mechanical condition, using two pieces of safety equipment (a rear-view mirror and a helmet), being aware of the most common biking hazards, and not riding at night unless prepared for it.

Before going out for a ride, be sure your bike is mechanically sound. Its condition is especially important if you bought the bike at a discount store, where it was probably assembled by a high school kid with no training. Above all, be sure that the wheels are secure and the brakes work.

Invest in a rear-view mirror and a bicycle helmet, both available at any bike shop. The mirror attaches to your glasses, your helmet, or your handlebars, and works like a charm when properly adjusted. Its greatest asset is that when you come to an obstacle, such as a pothole or a patch of broken glass, you can tell at a glance whether or not it's safe to swing out into the road to avoid it. On narrow or winding roads you can always be aware of the traffic behind you and plan accordingly. Best of all, a mirror eliminates the need to peek back over your shoulder—an action not only awkward but also potentially dangerous, because you sometimes unconsciously veer toward the middle of the road while peeking.

A bicycle helmet is the cyclist's cheapest form of life insurance. A helmet not only protects your head if you land on it after a fall, but also protects against the sun and the rain. More and more cyclists are wearing them, and so you shouldn't feel afraid of being thought a weirdo if you use one. Once you get used to a helmet you'll never even know you have one on.

While on the road, use the same plain old common sense that you use while driving. Stop signs and traffic lights are there for a reason—obey them. At intersections, give cars the benefit of the doubt rather than trying to dash in front of them or beat them through the light. Remember, they're bigger, heavier, and faster than you are. And you're out to enjoy yourself and get some exercise, not to be king of the road.

Several situations are inconsequential to the motorist, but potentially hazardous for the bicyclist. When biking, try to keep aware of these:

1. Road surface. Most roads in Rhode Island are not silk-smooth. Often the bicyclist must contend with bumps, ruts, cracks, potholes, and fish-scale sections of road that have been patched and repatched numerous times. When the road becomes rough, the only prudent course of action is to slow down and keep alert, especially going downhill. Riding into a deep pothole or wheel-swallowing crack can cause a nasty spill. On bumps, you can relieve some of the shock by getting up off the seat.

2. Sand patches. Patches of sand often build up at intersections, sharp curves, the bottom of hills, and sudden dips in the road. Sand is very unstable if you're turning, so slow way down, stop pedaling, and keep in a straight line until you're beyond the sandy spot.

3. Storm-sewer grates. Federal regulations have outlawed thousands of hazardous substances and products, but unfortunately have not yet outlawed the storm sewer with grates parallel to the roadway. This is a very serious hazard, because a cyclist catching the wheel in a slot will instantly fall, probably in a somersault over the handlebars. Storm sewers are relatively rare in rural areas, but always a very real hazard.

4. Dogs. Unfortunately, man's best friend is the cyclist's worst enemy. When riding in the country you will encounter dogs, pure and simple. Even though many communities have leash laws, they are usually not enforced unless a dog really mangles someone or annoys its owners' neighbors enough that they complain—a rare situation because the neighbors probably all have dogs, too.

The best defense against a vicious dog is to carry repellent— either ammonia in a squirtgun or plant sprayer (make sure it is leakproof), or a commercial dog spray called Halt, which comes in an aerosol can and is available at most bike shops. Repellent is effective only if you can grab it instantly when you need it—*don't* put it in your handlebar pack, a deep pocket, or any place else where you'll have to fish around for it. For Halt to work you have to squirt it directly into the dog's eyes, but if the dog is close enough to really threaten you it's easily done.

The main danger from dogs is not being bitten, but rather bumping into them or instinctively veering toward the center of the road into oncoming traffic when the dog comes after you. Fortunately, almost all dogs have a sense of territory and will not chase you more than a tenth of a mile. If you're going along at a brisk pace in front of the dog when it starts to chase you, you can probably outrun it and stay ahead until you reach the animal's territorial limit. If you are going at a leisurely pace, however, or heading uphill, or the dog is in the road in front of you, the only safe thing to do is dismount and walk slowly forward, keeping the bike between you and the dog, until you leave its territory. If the dog is truly menacing, or there's more than one, repellent can be comforting to have.

If you decide to stay on the bike when a dog chases you, always get into low gear and spin your legs as quickly as possible. It's hard for a dog to bite a fast-rotating target. Many cyclists swing their pump at the animal, but this increases the danger of losing control of your bike. Often, yelling "Stay!" or "No!" in an authoritative voice will make a dog back off.

5. Undivided, shoulderless four-lane highways. This is the most dangerous type of road for biking. If traffic is very light there is no problem, but in moderate or heavy traffic the road becomes a death trap unless you ride assertively. The only safe way to travel on such a road is to stay in or near the center of the right lane, rather than at the edge, forcing traffic coming up behind you to pass you in the left lane. If you hug the right-hand edge, some motorists will not get out of the right lane, brushing past you by inches or even forcing you off the road. Some drivers mentally register a bicycle as being only as wide as its tire, an unsettling image when the lane is not much wider than a car.

Several rides in this book contain short stretches along highways. If traffic is heavy enough to occupy both lanes most of the time, the only truly safe thing to do is walk your bike along the side of the road.

6. Railroad tracks. Tracks that cross the road at an oblique angle are a severe hazard, because you can easily catch your wheel in the slot between the rails and fall. NEVER ride diagonally across tracks—either walk your bike across, or, if no traffic is in sight, cross the tracks at right angles by swerving into the road. When riding across tracks, slow down and get up off the seat to relieve the shock of the bump.

7. Oiled and sanded roads. Many communities spread a film of oil or tar over the roads in the fall to seal cracks before winter. Then they spread sand over the road to absorb the oil. The combination is treacherous for biking. Be very careful, especially going downhill. If the tar or oil is still wet, better walk or you'll never get your bike clean.

8. Car doors opening into your path. This is a severe hazard in urban areas and in the center of towns. To be safe, any time you ride past a line of parked cars, stay four or five feet away from them. If oncoming traffic won't permit this, proceed very slowly and notice whether the driver's seat of each car is occupied. A car pulling to the side of the road in front of you is an obvious candidate for trouble.

9. Low sun. If you're riding directly into a low sun, traffic behind you may not see you, especially through a smeared or dirty windshield. Here your rear-view mirror becomes a lifesaver, because the only safe way to proceed is to glance constantly in the mirror and remain aware of conditions behind you. If you are riding directly away from a low sun, traffic coming toward you may not see you and could make a left turn into your path. If the sun is on your right or left, drivers on your side may not see you, and a car could pull out from a side road into your path. To be safe, give any traffic that may be blinded by the sun the benefit of the doubt, and dismount if necessary. Because most of the roads you'll be on are winding and wooded, you won't run into blinding sun frequently, but you should remain aware of the problem.

10. Kids on bikes. Little kids riding their bikes in circles in the middle of the road and shooting in and out of driveways are a hazard: the risk of collision is always there because they aren't watching where they're going. Any time you see kids playing in the street, especially if they're on bikes, be prepared for anything and call out "Beep-beep" or "Watch out" as you approach. If you have a loud bell or horn, use it.

11. Wet leaves. In the fall, wet leaves are very slippery. Avoid turning on them.

12. Metal-grate bridges. When wet, the metal grating becomes very slippery, and you may be in danger of falling and injuring yourself on the sharp edges. If the road is wet, or early in the morning when there may be condensation on the bridge, please walk across.

A few additional safety reminders: If bicycling in a group, ride single file and at least 20 feet apart. Use hand signals when turning—to signal a right turn, stick out your right arm. If you stop to rest or examine your bike, get both your bicycle and yourself completely off the road. Sleek black bicycle clothing is stylish, but bright colors are more visible and safer.

Finally, use common courtesy toward motorists and pedestrians. Hostility toward bicyclists has received national media attention; it is caused by the two percent who are discourteous cyclists (mainly messengers and groups hogging the road), who give the other 98 percent—responsible riders—a bad image. Please do not be part of the two percent!

The Narragansett Bay Wheelmen

If you would like to bike with a group and meet other people who enjoy cycling, the Narragansett Bay Wheelmen (NBW), which is the main bicycle club for the Rhode Island area, welcomes you on any of its rides. The club holds its rides on Sunday mornings. The rides include both the tours in this book and others a little farther into Massachusetts and Connecticut. You ride at your own pace and there is never any pressure of competition to ride farther or faster than you wish. There is always a short ride of under 20 miles if you don't want to tackle the longer ride. You can't get lost because for every ride, arrows are painted on the road at the turns, and maps are handed out.

Rides are announced in the Weekend section of the Providence paper on Fridays. You don't have to be a member to ride with the NBW, but the dues are nominal and by joining you get the club's bimonthly publication, The Spoke 'n Word, which lists upcoming rides for a couple months in advance and contains articles and news of the local biking scene. For more information, write to the NBW at P.O. Box 1317, Providence, RI 02901.

Other Organizations

Warwick Bicycle Club. This is a smaller and more informal club than the Narragansett Bay Wheelmen. Rides are generally 10 to 20 miles long, and announced in the Weekend section of the Providence paper on Fridays. For more information, ask at either Caster's or D.J. Handlbars bike shop in Warwick, or attend a ride.

Rhode Island Bicycle Coalition, P.O. Box 4781, Rumford, RI 02916. A political action group devoted to improving conditions for bicyclists. Projects include publication of a bicycle commuter map, replacement of unsafe sewer grates, bicycle safety education, and striving for bicycle access on the Newport Bridge.

Pequot Cyclists, Box 505, Gales Ferry, CT 06335. Based in southeastern Connecticut, with some rides in southwestern Rhode Island.

Quinebaug Valley Wheelmen. Based in the Putnam-Danielson area of Connecticut, with some rides in northwestern Rhode Island. For more information, inquire at the Ordinary Bike Shop in Danielson or the Silver Bike Shop in Putnam.

League of American Wheelmen, Suite 209, 6707 Whitestone Road, Baltimore, MD 21203. The main national organization of and for bicyclists. Excellent monthly magazine, dynamic legislative action program.

Feedback

I'd be grateful for any comments, criticisms, or suggestions about the rides in this book. Road conditions change, and a road that is safe to ride on now many resemble a lunar landscape in a couple of years. A new snack bar may open up along one of the routes. An intersection may be changed by road construction of improvement, or a traffic light may be installed. I'd like to keep the book updated by incorporating changes as they occur, or modifying a route if necessary in the interest of safety. Please feel free to contact me through The Globe Pequot Press, 138 West Main Street, Chester, CT 06412 with any revision you think helpful.

Further Reading and Resources

Metropolitan Providence Bicycle Map, by the Rhode Island Bicycle Coalition. Published 1983. Developed primarily for bicycle commuters but useful for any cyclist, the map rates all major streets in Providence and surrounding communities as good, acceptable, difficult, or dangerous for biking. Available from the RIBC (address given earlier). Free.

Rhode Island State Highway Map. Shows every back road. Describes points of interest and historic sites on back. Available from the Rhode Island Department of Economic Development, 7 Jackson Walkway, Providence RI 02903. Free.

Short Bike Rides in Greater Boston and Central Massachusetts, by Howard Stone. Second edition. Chester, CT: The Globe Pequot Press, 1988. One hundred and eight rides covering most of Massachusetts between the Cape Cod Canal and the Connecticut River.

Short Bike Rides on Cape Cod, Nantucket and the Vineyard, by Jane Griffith and Edwin Mullen. Third edition. Chester, CT: The Globe Pequot Press, 1984. Thirty rides.

Bicycle Touring in the Pioneer Valley, by Nancy Jane. Amherst, MA: University of Massachusetts Press, 1978. Sixteen rides.

Short Bike Rides in Connecticut, by Jane Griffith and Edwin Mullen. Second edition. Chester, CT: The Globe Pequot Press, 1984. Thirty rides.

Twenty-five Bicycle Tours in New Hampshire, by Tom and Susan Heavey. Revised edition. Woodstock, VT: Backcountry Publications, 1985.

Twenty-five Bicycle Tours in Vermont, by John Freidin. Woodstock, VT: Backcountry Publications, 1984.

Twenty-five Bicycle Tours in Maine, by Howard Stone. Woodstock, VT: Backcountry Publications, 1986.

New England over the Handlebars: A Cyclist's Guide, by Michael H. Farny. Boston: Little, Brown, 1975.

1. Tri–State Tour:
Pascoag—Douglas—Webster—Sutton

Number of miles: 18 (33 with Tri-state extension)

Terrain: Rolling, with one tough hill. The long ride has an additional hill.

Start: Supermarket in Pascoag, one block north of junction of Routes 107 and 100.

Food: None on short ride until end. Friendly Ice Cream, corner of Routes 12, 193, and 16, Webster. Small grocery at Sutton Falls Campground, Manchaug Road, Sutton, open during camping season.

This is a tour of the mostly wooded and lake-studded countryside surrounding the point where Rhode Island, Connecticut, and Massachusetts meet. The terrain is not as hilly as in the areas to the south and west. The lightly travelled back roads, winding through woods and along several ponds, promise enjoyable and peaceful bicycling.

The ride starts from the attractive little mill town of Pascoag, in the northwestern corner of the state. With massive granite and brick mills straight from the Industrial Revolution, Pascoag is typical of the many mill villages hugging the fast-flowing rivers throughout Rhode Island. Unfortunately, its largest mill burned to the ground in 1980. Leaving Pascoag, skirt the Wilson Reservoir and climb gradually to the top of Buck Hill, one of Rhode Island's highest points, with an elevation of 730 feet.

The ride down the western side is a thriller. After another hill descend steeply into the northeastern corner of Connecticut, into the town of Thompson, best known for its automobile race track, the Thompson Speedway. After about three miles of narrow lanes, cross the Massachusetts state line into Webster, a small and rather bleak mill city. As you head toward town on Route 193, you'll follow the shore of Lake Chargoggagoggmanchaugagoggchaubunagungamaug, which in the Nipmuc Indian language means, "I fish on my side, you fish on your side, and nobody fishes in the middle." If it hasn't been stolen, a sign spelling out the name of the lake greets you as you cross the state line.

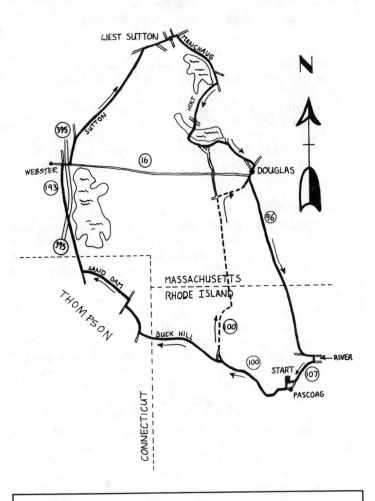

How to get there: Take Route 44 to Chepachet. Bear right on Route 102 (from the west, turn sharp left). Just ahead, go straight on Route 100 for 3 miles to Route 107. Turn right and take first left. Supermarket is opposite the far end of street.

Directions for the ride: 33 miles

- Right out of parking lot for one block to end (Route 100).
- Turn right. After 100 yards main road turns 90 degrees right. Go 3.2 miles to Buck Hill Road, which bears left (sign may say to Zambarano Hospital). Here the short ride goes straight.
- Bear left for 0.1 mile to fork.
- Bear left for 3 miles to end (merge right at bottom of second long downhill). **Caution:** Both descents are steep and bumpy. Take it easy.
- Bear right for 1.2 miles to end. Go right 0.1 mile to fork.
- Bear left on Sand Dam Road for 2 miles to end.
- Bear right on Route 193 for 3 miles to third traffic light (Routes 16 and 12).
- Right for 0.3 mile to Sutton Road, just past Route 395 underpass.
- Left on Sutton Road for 0.3 mile to where it turns right; go right for 3.8 miles to end.
- Right for 0.2 mile to fork (main road bears slightly left downhill).
- Bear left for one mile to second right (Manchaug Road), which is almost at bottom of long downhill (sign may say Sutton Falls Campground).
- Right for 2.3 miles to fork; Torrey Road goes straight down steep hill. Follow it for 0.3 mile to Holt Road, at pond.
- Right for 1.3 miles to fork (Wallis Street bears right).
- Bear right (do not turn sharp right), and cycle for 1.2 miles to another fork. There is 0.1 mile of dirt road when you cross the pond.
- Bear slightly left, and cycle for 0.7 mile to end (merge right; no stop sign).
- Bear right at end, and cycle for 0.6 mile to fork; bear left on main road, and cycle for 0.4 mile to another fork (church on right).
- Bear right for 0.1 mile into Route 16. Just ahead Route 16 turns right, but go straight for 50 yards to fork.
- Bear left on Route 96 for 6.6 miles to stop sign where main road bears left. Continue 0.1 mile to River Street on right.
- Right for 0.1 mile to end (Route 107).
- Right for 1.4 miles to end and supermarket, staying on main road.

Directions for the ride: 18 miles

- Follow first 2 directions of long ride.
- Straight on Route 100. After 2.2 miles, road curves 90 degrees left. Go 3.1 miles to crossroads and stop sign.
- Right for 1.3 miles to end (merge left on Route 96 at top of short hill). Douglas just ahead.
- Sharp right for 6.6 miles to stop sign where main road bears left. Continue 0.1 mile to River Street on right.
- Follow last 2 directions of long ride.

Skirting the edge of Webster quickly head into rolling, wooded countryside to the tiny village of West Sutton. Here you will pass Sutton Falls, a small dam with a little covered bridge above it. Just ahead are pleasant runs along Manchaug Pond, the Whitin Reservoir, and the graceful, classic New England village of Douglas, marked by a stately white church, old cemetery, and triangular green. From Douglas follow a smooth secondary road, Route 96, back to Pascoag.

The short ride bypasses Buck Hill and Connecticut by heading north directly into Massachusetts. Just before the state line is Zambarano Hospital, a state institution for the severely retarded and handicapped. Behind the hospital is Wallum Lake, half in Rhode Island and half in Massachusetts. You climb sharply onto a wooded ridge that parallels the lake and then follow a country lane through deep forests into Douglas, where you pick up Route 96 for the return trip to Pascoag.

2. Burrillville

Number of miles: 16 (26 with Pascoag extension)
Terrain: Rolling, with some short hills.
Start: Dino's Park and Shop Supermarket, Route 44, Chepachet.
Food: Grocery stores and small restaurants in the mill villages.

On this ride you'll explore the northwestern corner of Rhode Island, a fascinating area of woods, ponds, and mill villages tucked in valleys along swift-moving streams. Bicycling is fun on the numerous back roads that twist through the forest from one village to the next. The town of Burrillville contains seven distinct communities, all of which you'll pass through if you take the longer ride.

The ride starts from Chepachet, a town in Glocester just south of the Burrillville line, containing some handsome early nineteenth-century homes. As you leave town, you pass Old Chepachet Village, a combination gift shop, restaurant, and natural-foods store. Head northeast on Old Route 102, which connects the four mill villages of Mapleville, Oakland, Glendale, and Nasonville, evenly spaced about a mile apart along the Chepachet and Branch Rivers. You'll have this road nearly to yourself, since almost all the traffic will be on fast, straight New Route 102.

The first community you come to, Mapleville, is the largest of the four. Its houses, closely spaced along the road, comprise a fascinating mixture of architectural styles, ranging from traditional mill-village duplexes with peaked roofs to rambling homes with broad porches. There are two fine churches, the first one of stone, and the second one of both stone and wood. The next three villages are smaller and more rundown, with rows of identical wooden houses, originally built for the workers, flanking the stone or red-brick mills. In Nasonville, the Western Hotel, a marvelous, long wooden building with a porch along its entire front, guards the corner of Old Route 102 and Route 7. Across the street are a country store and a former Victorian schoolhouse with a bell tower, tastefully remodeled into apartments.

Turn northwest on Route 7 and pass through Mohegan, with its

27

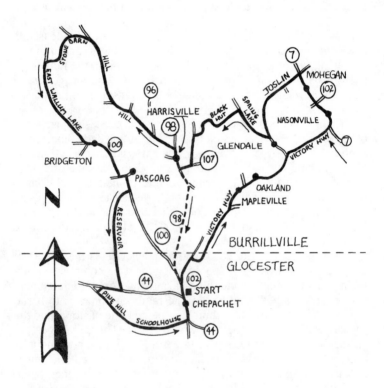

How to get there: Exit west from Route 295 onto Route 44. Supermarket is about 8 miles ahead on right.

Directions for the ride: 26 miles

- Right out of parking lot for 0.2 mile to fork.
- Bear right on Route 102 for 0.1 mile to where Route 102 bears right. Continue on Route 102 for 0.9 mile to unmarked road which bears right parallel to main road. (This is Old Route 102, Victory Highway.)
- Bear right for 1.7 miles to fork with garage in middle.
- Bear left for 0.4 mile to another fork.
- Straight (don't bear left) for 1.8 miles to another fork. Take right-hand branch over a small bridge, and then go straight on main road for 0.9 mile to end (blinking light at bottom of hill, Route 7).
- Bear left for 0.3 mile to traffic light (Route 102).
- Straight for 0.8 mile to crossroads (Joslin Road).
- Left for 1.2 miles to Spring Lake Road, while going down steep hill; take sharp right for 1.3 miles to Black Hut Road on left, which passes between two stone pillars.
- Left for 1.6 miles to end (Cherry Farm Road).
- Left for 0.6 mile to end; merge right on Route 107 and go 0.1 mile to end (Main Street, Route 98). Here the short ride turns left.
- Right for 0.3 mile to second left (Route 96, School Street).
- Left for 0.4 mile to where main road bears right and smaller road goes straight.
- Straight for 0.4 mile to fork where Hill Road bears left. Follow it for 0.7 mile to fork where Hill Road bears right.
- Bear right for 1.4 miles to another fork where Hill Road goes straight.
- Bear left on Stone Barn Road for 0.4 mile to fork, and bear left (still Stone Barn Road) for 0.7 miles to end. Left for 2.3 miles to end (merge left into Route 100). **Caution:** Bumpy downhill stretch. Take it easy.
- Bear left for 0.9 mile to end. Follow main road left downhill for one block where Route 100 turns right.
- Right for 0.2 mile to Reservoir Road.
- Right for 2.4 miles to end (Route 44).
- Right for a half mile to Pine Orchard Road, a narrow lane that bears left. Follow it 0.1 mile to paved road.
- Sharp left for 2.9 miles to end (Route 44).
- Left for 0.3 mile to parking lot on right.

Directions for the ride: 16 miles

- Follow first 10 directions of long ride, to Route 98.
- Left on Route 98 for 0.2 mile to fork; bear right on Route 98 for 2.4 miles to end.
- Bear left on Route 100 for 0.9 mile to end (merge left on Route 44).
- Bear left for 0.2 mile to parking lot on left.

row of mill houses in varying need of repair straggling up the hillside. Just after you cross New Route 102, a road on your right leads up a short steep hill to the Shrine of the Little Flowers, from which there's a fine view. The route now heads west along narrow wooded roads toward Harrisville, the most attractive of Burrillville's communities. You'll pass Spring Lake, nestled in the woods and flanked by a cluster of summer cottages. As you arrive in Harrisville, you'll see a beautiful dam and a complex of nineteenth-century brick and stone mills. A traditional white New England church stands above the dam and millpond, and in the next block, is another stately church, this one of brick. The short ride now heads back to Chepachet along Route 98, a smooth secondary road that passes through a stretch of open fields.

The long ride heads northwest along narrow lanes to a very rural area. Small farms with rustic barns and stone walls punctuate the wooded hillsides. Descend to the Wilson Reservoir and arrive in Bridgeton, where there's a wonderful, red wooden schoolhouse with a graceful bell tower. Bridgeton blends into Pascoag, the largest of Burrillville's villages. Just out of town, a relaxing run goes along the slender Pascoag Reservoir. The last two miles are mostly downhill as you wind along a small wooded lane with two ponds.

3. Warwick—Cranston—Roger Williams Park

Number of miles: 14
Terrain: Flat with a couple of short hills.
Start: Howard Johnson's, Jefferson Boulevard, Warwick.
Food: Several stores and restaurants on the route. Howard
   Johnson's at end.

On this ride you'll explore the two residential suburbs just south of
Providence. Although built up, the region is much more pleasant for
biking than you might think, as long as you stay off the numerous
four-lane arteries that slash through the two cities.

The ride starts in the heart of Warwick, which can only be
described as the archetypical American suburb. It is best known for
the massive Warwick-Rhode Island Mall shopping complex (the
largest in Rhode Island), T. F. Green State Airport, and bumper-to-
bumper traffic on Interstate 95—none of which you'll be biking
near. Beyond lies a much more appealing community of quiet tree-
lined streets and small peninsulas jutting into Narragansett Bay.

The first few miles of the ride wind along residential streets
past modest single-family homes typical of most of Warwick. As
you approach the bay, you pass through the affluent subdivision of
Governor Francis Farms, with sprawling homes overlooking large,
well-trimmed lawns. Head north on Narragansett Parkway, a gently
curving boulevard paralleling the bay with gracious older homes on
both sides. You'll pass a waterfront park on your right where every
June thousands of spectators watch a re-enactment of the 1772
burning of the British revenue schooner, *Gaspee*, by Rhode Island
patriots. Continue on to another bayside park with a gazebo, which
marks Pawtuxet Village. This historic community, which straddles
both sides of the Pawtuxet River, forms the border between Warwick
and Cranston. The village comes alive when it hosts Gaspee Days, a
week-long celebration every June commemorating the burning of
the *Gaspee*.

On the Cranston side of the village you bike along the head of
boat-filled Pawtuxet Cove that forms the mouth of the river, and
then proceed to the tip of Pawtuxet Neck, a slender peninsula lined

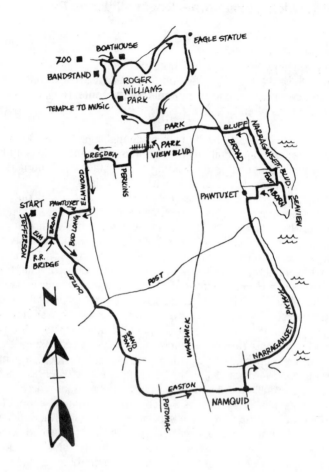

How to get there: The start is immediately east of I-95. Take the Jefferson Boulevard Exit (no. 15). By bike from Providence, head south on Elmwood Avenue to where Reservoir Avenue bears right. Continue straight for 3 miles to Pawtuxet Avenue on right, at traffic light. Follow last 3 directions of ride.

Directions for the ride

- Left out of parking lot on Jefferson Boulevard for 0.2 mile to Elm Street; bear left for one short block to end.
- Turn left. Just ahead is small railroad bridge on right. *Walk* bike across bridge, which is one way in wrong direction.
- Bear right on far side of bridge. Go 0.2 mile to Outlet Avenue.
- Bear right for one short block to stop sign; bear left for 0.3 mile to traffic light (Post Road).
- Jog left and immediately right on Sand Pond Road for 0.2 mile to crossroads and stop sign. Notice Sand Pond on left.
- Go straight, and immediately bear left at fork (still Sand Pond Road). Go 0.2 mile to where Sand Pond Road bears left. Bear left and cycle 100 yards to another fork.
- Bear right (still Sand Pond Road) for 0.3 mile to crossroads and stop sign (Potomac Road).
- Straight on Easton Avenue for a half mile to traffic light (Warwick Avenue).
- Straight on Namquid Drive for 0.7 mile to rotary.
- Left for 0.3 mile to stop sign (Narragansett Parkway).
- Right for 1.7 miles to traffic light; go straight. (Just before light, short dead-end roads on right go to Pawtuxet Cove.) Just ahead is bridge over Pawtuxet River; right on Aborn Street just after bridge. After 100 yards street turns 90 degrees left. Go another 100 yards to end. (To see Rhodes-on-the-Pawtucket, continue straight past bridge to third left and turn left on Rhodes Street.)
- Right for 0.1 mile to end (Fort Avenue).
- Right for 0.1 mile to Seaview Avenue on left. Left for 0.2 mile to end (tip of Pawtuxet Neck).
- Backtrack to Fort Avenue. Right for a quarter mile to end.
- Turn left, then immediately bear right along bay on Narragansett Boulevard. Go a half mile to Bluff Avenue, after house number 1373.
- Left for 0.3 mile to end (Broad Street).
- Jog right and immediately left on Park Avenue. Go 0.3 mile to traffic light (Warwick Avenue).
- Straight for a half mile to entrance to Roger Williams Park on right, at traffic light.
- Right into park for 100 yards to end. Left for 0.6 mile to fork after Temple to Music.

- Bear right on main road for 100 yards to another fork.
- Bear left downhill for 0.2 mile to end (merge left just before little bridge). Notice bandstand on left.
- Turn right. (To visit zoo, bear left.) After little bridge curve left at fork for 0.3 mile to another fork at top of hill.
- Bear right for a half mile to fork with eagle statue in middle.
- Bear right for 0.6 mile to fork. Bear right again, following pond on right. Go 0.6 mile to park exit on left at bottom of hill.
- Turn left out of park and cross Park Avenue at traffic light onto Park View Boulevard. Go 0.4 mile to railroad tracks. Ciba-Geigy plant is on left.
- Right immediately after tracks for 0.2 mile to Dresden Street.
- Right for one block. Continue straight for 0.4 mile to busy crossroads and stop sign (Elmwood Avenue).
- Left for 0.6 mile to traffic light (Pawtuxet Avenue).
- Bear right for 0.3 mile to fork (Budlong Avenue turns left); bear right for 100 yards to first left (Broad Street).
- Left for 0.3 mile to first right. Right across small railroad bridge. Bear left immediately after bridge on Walnut Street. Go 100 yards to Elm Street on right.
- Right on Elm St. for 100 yards to end (Jefferson Boulevard). Bear right for 0.2 mile to Howard Johnson's.

with handsome homes. Head north along the bay through the Edgewood section of Cranston, where Narragansett Boulevard, a broad tree-lined avenue of rambling older homes, is a pleasure for biking. A couple of blocks off the route is a fond landmark, Rhodes-on-the-Pawtuxet, one of New England's last remaining ballroom dance halls in the grand Victorian tradition.

A mile inland from the bay you enter Roger Williams Park, one of America's finest nineteenth-century urban parks. Meticulously landscaped, it features several ponds, a zoo, flower gardens, gazebos, bandstands, and an impressive collection of ornate Victorian buildings, including a museum of natural history. Here is the loveliest landmark of all, the marble-columned Temple to Music. Built in the style of a Greek temple, the graceful white monument stands on the lakeshore fronted by a broad, gently sloping lawn.

The recent restoration of the park to its original resplendence is one of Rhode Island's success stories. Ten years ago the park was a littered, neglected remnant of its former self. Under the dynamic leadership of a new parks superintendent, James Diamond, a sustained effort was begun in the late 1970s to re-landscape and maintain the grounds, improve the zoo, and restore the buildings. Tragically, Diamond was fired in 1983 because of his outspokenness and disagreements with the mayor of Providence. One can only wonder whether the park will once again sink into neglect and decay.

After leaving Roger Williams Park, it's a few miles through residential neighborhoods back to the starting point. You can catch a glimpse of the massive Ciba-Geigy chemical plant, conveniently located on the bank of the Pawtuxet River, which it sometimes uses as a disposal area. The factory, a source of controversy because of its refusal to install pollution-control systems, is being phased out. Cross the river back into Warwick.

4. Cumberland—Wrentham–Plainville

Number of miles: 18 (29 with Plainville loop, 10 with shortcut)
Terrain: Rolling to hilly, with two big downhill runs on the longer ride.
Start: Diamond Hill State Park, Route 114, Cumberland.
Food: Grocery at corner of Route 121 and Hancock Street, Wrentham. Burger King, corner of Routes 106 and 152, Plainville. Ice cream at end opposite entrance to park.

This ride explores the rural, largely wooded area surrounding the northeast corner of the state. You can amble along at a leisurely pace to savor the beauty of the narrow, twisting back roads. At the end of the ride is a delightful run along the Diamond Hill Reservoir.

The ride starts from Diamond Hill State Park, marked by a cliff of veined quartz over two hundred feet high, a favorite spot for rock climbers. The park once contained a ski area, but the unpredictable snowfall of the Rhode Island winter made its continued operation unprofitable. Sunday afternoon concerts are a tradition at the park's amphitheatre. The first few miles of the ride climb gradually on Route 120, passing Sneech Pond. You will be rewarded with a smooth descent on West Wrentham Road through open farmland with fine views.

About seven miles from the starting point you cross the state line into Wrentham, Massachusetts, a gracious town of small farms, horse pastures, and well-maintained homes. Although technically within the Boston metropolitan area, the community is far enough from the city to have a rural, rather than suburban, atmosphere. Spring Street, a narrow winding lane, bobs up and over several sharp hills, none long enough to be discouraging. You can stop for a breather at the country store in Sheldonville, a village within Wrentham. Notice the stately white church just past the store.

Ahead is the town of Plainville, which lies just east of the Rhode Island border. This town is similar to Wrentham, but a little more built up because of its proximity to Providence and the Attleboros. You will pass a branch of the Wentworth Institute, an engineering school whose main campus is in Boston. You cross back

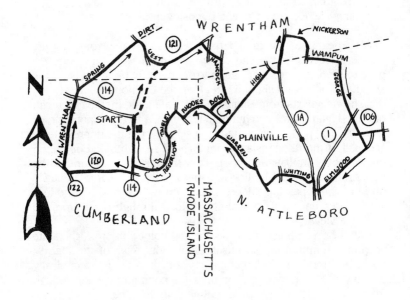

How to get there: From Route 295, exit north on Route
114 and go about 4 miles to parking lot on right. By bike
from Providence, head north on North Main Street. At
Pawtucket line bear left on Route 122 (Main Street).
Follow Route 122 for about 5 miles to Marshall Avenue
on right. Right for 0.6 mile to end (Route 114). Left for
about 6 miles to parking lot on right.

Directions for the ride: 29 miles

- Left out of parking lot for 1.4 miles to traffic light (Route 120, Nate Whipple Highway). Note: 10-mile ride turns right out of lot instead of left.
- Right on Route 120 for 2.5 miles to end (Route 122, Mendon Road). Right for 0.2 mile to West Wrentham Road (sign may say to Resurrection Cemetery).
- Right for 2.4 miles to crossroads and stop sign (Route 114); straight for 0.1 mile to fork.
- Bear right for 2 miles to crossroads (dirt road goes straight); right for 0.9 mile to end (Route 121).
- Left for 1.3 miles to Hancock Street (country store on corner).
- Right for 0.2 mile to diagonal crossroads and go straight for a half mile to end, at top of hill.
- Right (still Hancock Street) for 1.1 mile to Bow Street on right.
- Right for a half mile to end (Rhodes Street). Here the 18-mile ride turns right.
- Left for 0.6 mile to end (High Street).
- Left for 1.4 mile to stop sign (main road bears left, Green Street turns right). There is a sand and gravel plant at the intersection.
- Right for 0.2 mile to end (Route 1A).
- Left for 0.7 mile to Nickerson Lane, just before Route 495. Right for 0.7 mile to first left (Wampum Street, unmarked).
- Turn left. After 0.6 mile main road turns 90 degrees right. Continue for 1.4 miles to Route 1.
- Straight for a half mile to Route 106. **Caution:** Watch out for Route 1 traffic. (For Burger King turn left on Route 106 for 0.4 mile.) Go straight for 0.1 mile to end (Elmwood Road).
- Right for 1.5 miles to traffic light (Routes 1 and 1A).
- Straight across Route 1 at light, then immediately right on Route 1A. Be sure you're on Route 1A and not Route 1. Go 100 yards to Whiting Street.
- Left for 1.1 miles to end. (The road turns sharply and crosses two side roads, but stay on it to end.)
- Right for 0.3 mile to Warren Street.
- Left for 1.2 miles to end.
- Right for 0.3 mile to Rhodes Street.
- Left for 1.3 miles to end (Burnt Swamp Road).

- Right for 0.3 mile to end.
- Left on Tingley Road for 2.5 miles to end (Route 114). **Caution:** First ¾ mile bumpy; go slow on descent to reservoir.
- Right for 0.9 mile to park entrance on right.

Directions for the ride: 18 miles
- Follow first 8 directions of long ride to Rhodes Street.
- Right for 0.7 mile to end (Burnt Swamp Road).
- Follow last 3 directions of long ride.

Directions for the ride: 10 miles
- Right out of parking lot for 0.2 mile to end.
- Right on Route 121 for 2.8 miles to Hancock Street on right (country store on corner).
- Right for 0.2 mile to diagonal crossroads. Straight for a half mile to end, at top of hill.
- Right (still Hancock Street) for 1.1 mile to Bow Street; right for a half mile to end (Rhodes Street).
- Follow last 3 directions of the 29-mile ride.

into Rhode Island and descend to the Diamond Hill Reservoir, which suddenly looms before you as you go around a sharp bend. The long, flat run along the shoreline is a refreshing contast to the rolling hills. Soon you come to Route 114, less than a mile from the starting point. The rugged cliffs of Diamond Hill are on your right as you approach the park entrance.

An exhilarating downhill run on the recently repaved High Street in Plainville begins the loop of the long ride. A few miles ahead you can stop for a bite at Burger King or McDonald's before tackling the steep ridge between Plainville and North Attleboro. At the top of the hill is World War I Memorial Park, which has a fire tower and a small zoo. A fast descent from the park provides your reward for the climb. After several more miles through woods and small farms, you rejoin the short ride in time for the run along the Diamond Hill Reservoir.

5. Ray Young's Ride:
Greenville—Chepachet—Mapleville

Number of miles: 19 (30 with Chepachet—Mapleville extension)
Terrain: Rolling, with several short sharp hills.
Start: IGA Supermarket, Route 44, Greenville.
Food: Grocery in Chepachet. Country store in Mapleville.
  Supermarket at end. McDonald's at junction of Routes 44
  and 5, one mile east of starting point.

This is a delightful ride along country lanes through the rolling and
very rural landscape of the northern quarter of Rhode Island. This
area is the state's prime apple-growing region, so the best time to
bike here is in the first half of May, when apple blossoms cover the
orchards in a delicate white canopy, or during harvest season in
October and early November, when you can stuff your saddlebags
full of apples right off the tree for pennies.

The village of Greenville in the town of Smithfield is an attractive place to begin the ride. Notice the handsome stone church in
the center of town. Within a mile you'll be in rolling orchard country, bobbing up and down small hills, none long enough to be discouraging. Peeptoad Road, across the town line in Scituate, is an
appealing lane winding past secluded country homes and an observatory belonging to the Skyscrapers, an amateur astronomy
club. A pristine little pond lies at the end of the road.

As you swing west and then north, the landscape becomes
more rural, with weathered barns and an occasional house tucked
away in the woods. A couple of longer climbs, counterbalanced by
fast descents on Snake Hill, Chestnut Oak, and Absalona Hill Roads,
bring you to Glocester, a thoroughly rural town dotted with lakes,
orchards, and small farms. The short route curves southward on
Evans Road, another narrow byway which seems to have been designed with the bicyclist in mind. If you use your gears efficiently
over one little knoll after another, each downhill run is long enough
to get you most of the way up the next short climb. The last mile
returns you to Greenville down a long gentle hill past the Saint
Aloysius Home, a Catholic home for disturbed children.

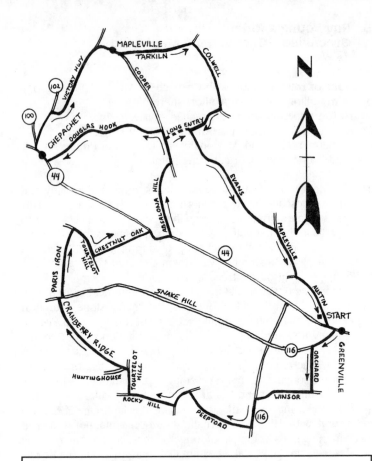

How to get there: From Route 295, exit west onto Route 44. Go about 2 miles to Route 116 on left in center of Greenville. IGA is just ahead on right. By bike from Providence, head west on Chalkstone Avenue. Cross bridge over small river into Johnston. Go 0.8 mile to second fork (Greenville Avenue bears left uphill). Bear left for 3 miles to where Greenville Avenue turns left downhill. Left for 1.4 miles to end (Route 44). Left for 0.2 mile to IGA on right.

Directions for the ride: 30 miles

- Left out of parking lot on Route 44 for 0.1 mile to traffic light (Route 116 on right). **Caution:** Watch for traffic.
- Right for 0.6 mile to Orchard Avenue, almost at top of hill.
- Left for 0.8 mile to end (Winsor Road).
- Right for one mile to Route 116.
- Bear left for 0.7 mile to Peeptoad Road.
- Make a sharp right for 1.4 miles to end.
- Left for 0.4 mile to Rocky Hill Road.
- Right for 1.1 miles to Tourtellot Hill Road.
- Right for 0.7 mile to Huntinghouse Road.
- Left for 0.2 mile to fork; bear right on Cranberry Ridge Road for 1.4 mile to end (Snake Hill Road).
- Right for 0.2 mile to Paris Iron Road.
- Left for 1.1 miles to end; right for a half mile to Chestnut Oak Road.
- Left for 1.2 miles to end (Route 44). (**Caution:** Steep downhill.)
- Right for a half mile to Absalona Hill Road.
- Left for 1.5 miles to end (Cooper Road). (**Caution:** making left turn.)
- Left for a half mile to Long Entry Road. Here the short ride turns right.
- Straight for 0.2 mile to Douglas Hook Road.
- Left for 2.7 miles to end (Route 44 in Chepachet).
- Right for 0.2 mile to fork.
- Bear right on Routes 102 and 100. Just ahead, Route 102 bears right and Route 100 goes straight. Bear right for 0.9 mile to Victory Highway (Old Route 102) on right.
- Right for 1.7 miles to fork with garage in middle.
- Bear right for 0.3 mile to Tarkiln Road.
- Bear left for 2.2 miles to fork.
- Bear right on Colwell Road for 0.8 mile to fork (main road bears left, golf course entrance bears right).
- Bear left for one mile to where the main road curves sharply left and Long Entry Road (unmarked) turns right.
- Turn right on Long Entry Road for one mile to Evans Road.
- Left for 3.7 miles to end, at T-intersection (Austin Avenue).
- Left for 1.3 miles to end (Route 44).
- Turn right. Parking lot is just ahead on right.

Directions for the ride: 19 miles

- Follow first 16 directions of long ride, to Long Entry Road.
- Right on Long Entry Road for 0.6 mile to fork.
- Bear right on Evans Road for 3.7 miles to end, at T-intersection (Austin Avenue).
- Left for 1.3 miles to end (Route 44). Turn right and IGA is just ahead on right.

The long ride heads farther northwest through more orchards to Chepachet, an attractive town of lovely houses, many dating back to around 1800. The town hosts a colorful Ancient and Horribles July 4th parade. Next you'll go through Mapleville, a mill village at the edge of Burrillville, the most northwesterly town in the state. With a pair of grim-looking brick mills flanked by a row of identical dwellings originally built for the workers, Mapleville is typical of the many small mill villages that dot Rhode Island. A narrow back road takes you past the expansive lawns of the Country View Golf Club to rejoin the short ride at Evans Road.

6. Smithfield—North Smithfield—Slatersville

Number of miles: 11 (27 with North Smithfield-Slatersville extension)

Terrain: Rolling, with one tough hill. The long ride has two additional hills.

Start: Small shopping center at junction of Route 5 and Log Road, Smithfield.

Food: None on route of short ride. Snack bars on Route 146A. Snack bar and country store in Nasonville. Pizza at end. McDonald's and Burger King at corner of Routes 5 and 44, two miles south of starting point.

The region northwest of Providence, midway between the city and the Massachusetts border, abounds with twisting secondary roads that provide enjoyable bicycling if you're willing to tackle an occasional hill. The landscape is primarily rolling woodland dotted with boulders, ponds, and picturesque mill villages. At several spots along the route, tumbling streams rush alongside or underneath the road.

Begin the ride in Smithfield, a town blending undeveloped woods and farmland, apple orchards, old mill villages, and some pockets of suburban growth. After leaving the parking lot immediately follow the shore of the unspoiled Woonasquatucket Reservoir on Log Road, and then cross the cascading Woonasquatucket River shortly before it flows into the reservoir.

The short ride now proceeds on Route 104 on the other side of the reservoir, passing the popular rock nightclub, Gulliver's. A mile ahead, turn onto a narrow side road that descends steeply into Stillwater, a lovely and classic mill village. Most of the stately wooden houses have been restored, but unfortunately the old brick mill was destroyed by fire several years ago. The road then ascends onto a ridge overlooking Georgiaville Pond before it drops into Georgiaville. This is another fine mill village, with three-story wood and stone houses, a large brick mill set back from the road, and the swift-flowing Woonasquatucket River darting through the town. Just past Esmond, the next mill village downstream, you will have

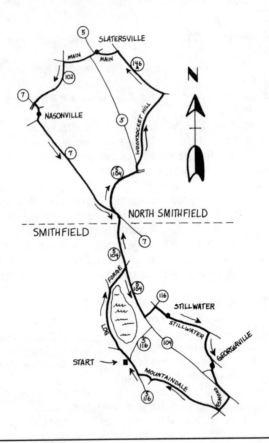

How to get there: From Route 295, exist west on Route 44 for ³/₄ mile to Route 5, at traffic light. Right for about 2 miles to parking lot on left, at fork where main road bears right and Log Road bears left. By bike from Providence: Head northwest on Smith Street to Route 104, at traffic light just after Route 15. Right for about 4 miles to Route 5 on left, while going downhill. Left for 0.6 mile to parking lot on right.

Directions for the ride: 27 miles

- Left out of parking lot and immediately bear left on Log Road. Go 0.2 mile to fork.
- Bear right for 1.3 miles to Forge Road, just after reservoir.
- Bear right for a half mile to Route 5. Here the short ride turns right.
- Left for 1.3 miles to stop sign (merge left on Route 7).
- Bear left for 0.2 mile to fork.
- Bear right on Routes 5 and 104 for 1.3 miles to crossroads.
- Left on Route 5 for 0.2 mile to Woonsocket Hill Road.
- Bear right for 2.8 miles to end (Route 146A).
- Left for 1.5 miles to Main Street, just after Great Road bears right at top of hill.
- Left on Main Street for 1.2 miles to end (merge left at Slatersville green).
- Bear left for 1.2 miles to wide crossroads (Route 102).
- Left for 1.4 miles to traffic light (Route 7). Wright's Farm, a great fried chicken restaurant, is on right after 0.8 mile.
- Left for 0.3 mile to fork where route 7 bears left at blinking light. Follow it for 4 miles to fork where Route 7 goes straight and Routes 5 and 104 bear right.
- Bear right for 2.6 miles to Route 116 on left.
- Left for 0.6 mile to small crossroads (Stillwater Road).
- Right for 1.6 miles to unmarked road (still Stillwater Road) on right, immediately after Meadow View Drive on left. Turn right. Just ahead the main road curves left and a side road goes straight; stay on main road for 0.6 mile to fork.
- Bear right downhill and cross small bridge at bottom. Go 0.2 mile to fork just after new apartments on left. (Homestead Avenue bears left.)
- Bear left for 0.3 mile to end (merge left on Route 104).
- Bear left for a half mile to Esmond Street.
- Right for 0.4 mile to crossroads and stop sign.
- Turn right and immediately bear left at fork on smaller road. Go a quarter mile to fork.
- Bear right on main road. After 1.5 miles, main road curves right downhill and smaller road bears left. Stay on main road for 0.4

mile down steep hill to where Spragueville Road turns left and main road bears right.

- Bear right for a quarter mile to end (Route 5).
- Right for a half mile to parking lot on left.

Directions for the ride: 11 miles

- Follow first 3 directions of long ride, to Route 5.
- Right for 1.4 miles to Route 116 on left.
- Follow last 10 directions of long ride, beginning "Left for 0.6 mile . . ."

to tackle the one tough hill of the ride on well-named Mountaindale Road. But at the top you'll be compensated by a thrilling descent to the shore of the Woonasquatucket Reservoir. Just ahead is Route 116, only a half mile from the end.

The long ride includes North Smithfield, which consists of wooded hills sprinkled with small ponds. After passing Primrose Pond, turn onto Woonsocket Hill Road, a twisting lane that ascends onto a ridge overlooking Woonsocket. You come around a sharp curve, and a sweeping view of the city unfolds before you, followed by a flying descent. Continue on into Slatersville, the finest traditional mill village in Rhode Island, with most of its buildings dating back to the early 1800s. There's a lovely white church standing above the triangular town green, a handsome, pillared town hall, followed by several imposing three-story stone buildings. A cluster of Victorian stone and brick mills lies in the steep valley below with an orderly row of traditional duplex mill houses beyond. A mile beyond the village, you will pass an impressive two-tiered dam on your left.

Turn southeast back toward Smithfield on Route 7, an excellent cycling road which bobs up and down small wooded hills and then plunges steeply in a thrilling descent. You rejoin the short ride about two miles before the village of Stillwater.

7. The Lincoln Woods Ride:
North Providence—Lincoln—Smithfield

Number of miles: 18
Terrain: Hilly.
Start: McDonald's, Branch Avenue, Providence, just west of Route
146, and one mile west of I-95.
Food: Snack bar at Lincoln Woods, open during the summer.
McDonald's at end.

Just northwest of Providence, the urban area thins out quickly into affluent suburban neighborhoods and rolling hills dotted with horse farms. A highlight of this ride is a spin through Lincoln Woods, a state park with a beach on Olney Pond.

The ride starts near the northernmost point of Providence, close to the mill village of Wanskuck. Its focal point is a massive brick mill with a tall clock tower, built in 1862, which currently houses small diversified industries. Across Branch Avenue lie wooden and brick duplex and triplex houses, originally built for the mill workers.

The landscape becomes suburban as soon as you leave the parking lot. Heading north on Woodward Road, one of the best ways to bike out of the city, you pass the broad lawns of Wanskuck Park before a steep climb into North Providence. This town is a typical bedroom community bisected by the main drag, Mineral Spring Avenue, a three-mile strip of stores, car dealers, and fastfood outlets. Many cyclists call it Miserable Spring Avenue. Don't worry—you won't be riding on it. North of this artery the land becomes much less densely populated.

Just ahead you will pass the Louisquisset Hills condominium development, one of Rhode Island's largest and one of the few condominium complexes that is genuinely attractive. It borders the Louisquisset Golf Course. Around the corner, you will pass a state police barracks with a tall radio tower behind it. Across the road is Lincoln Greyhound Park, which until a few years ago was a raceway for horses. Just ahead cruise downhill to the entrance of Lincoln Woods State Park.

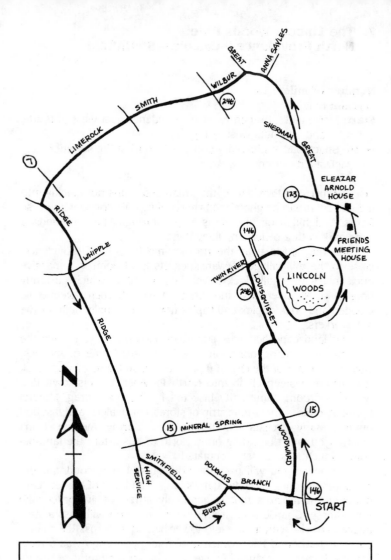

How to get there: The ride begins at McDonald's on Branch Avenue, just west of Route 146, and one mile west of I-95.

Directions for the ride

- Turn left out of parking lot on Branch Avenue, and immediately right on Woodward Road. Go 1.1 miles to traffic light (Mineral Spring Avenue).
- Straight for 0.9 mile to end (Route 246).
- Left for 1.2 miles to traffic light (Twin River Road).
- Right for 0.6 mile to end.
- Right for a half mile to fork. (Olney Pond on left.)
- Bear right on main road for 1.2 miles to end (stop sign).
- Right for 0.7 mile to end (Route 123).
- Left for a half mile to Great Road, which bears right. (To see Eleazar Arnold house, go right for 0.2 mile.)
- Right for 0.7 mile to fork (main road bears right, Sherman Avenue bears left).
- Bear right for 1.3 miles to fork at top of short hill.
- Bear left on Wilbur Road for 0.4 mile to crossroads and stop sign (Route 246).
- Straight up steep hill for 1.3 miles to crossroads (Route 123).
- Straight for 1.6 miles to crossroads (Route 7).
- Straight for 0.3 mile to Ridge Road on left (main road curves sharply right at intersection).
- Left for 0.9 mile to fork (Ridge Road bears right up steep hill). **Caution:** Bumpy downhill. Go slow.
- Bear right for 0.1 mile to crossroads (Whipple Road).
- Straight for 2.6 miles to traffic light (Mineral Spring Avenue).
- Straight on main road for 0.3 mile to fork.
- Bear left on Smithfield Road for 0.9 mile to Burns Street, just past bottom of big hill.
- Left for 0.3 mile to end (Douglas Avenue).
- Bear right on Branch Avenue (don't turn 90 degrees right on Douglas Avenue). Go 0.7 mile to McDonald's on right.

Lincoln Woods is a park Rhode Islanders can be proud of. Until two years ago the park was shabby, with a muddy little beach and roads so bumpy that biking was impossible. In 1981, the area received a complete facelift—the roads were repaved, grass was replanted, and the beach received a new bathhouse and layer of sand. The park is now a pleasure to bicycle through. The silk-smooth road hugs the shore of Olney Pond; then a swooping downhill run brings you to the park's north entrance, where you enter the Great Road Historic District.

Head northwest through a gracious area of elegant older homes, horse pastures, weathered barns, and small millponds with dams. Just off the route is the Eleazar Arnold House, built in 1687, which features a high-peaked roof and a massive stone chimney. It's open by appointment through the Society for the Preservation of New England Antiquities (617-227-3956). Just down the road is the Friends Meeting House. Built in 1703, it is the oldest Quaker meetinghouse in New England in continuous use.

Great Road ascends onto a ridge with fine views to the west; then you descend past a limestone quarry. The next few miles are on narrow, mostly wooded roads with some steep ups and downs. Just after you re-enter North Providence, you pass Peter Randall State Park, which could use a Lincoln Woods-style facelift. It has fallen into such complete neglect that the access road has been barricaded and covered with dirt to ward off vandalism. Opposite the former entrance, catch a glimpse of the Wenscott Reservoir, commonly known as Twin Rivers.

The fastest downhill run of the ride awaits as you cross the Providence city line. Just before you pull into the parking lot, you pass the Wanskuck Mill on your left.

8. Blackstone Valley Tour:
   Lincoln—Cumberland

Number of miles: 13 (24 with Cumberland loop)
Terrain: Hilly. To reward your efforts, however, there are several
   exciting downhill runs.
Start: McDonald's, Lincoln Mall, Route 116, Lincoln.
Food: Snack bar at beach in Lincoln Woods State Park, open
   during the summer. Grocery stores in Manville and Albion.
   Burger King on Route 122 in Cumberland.

This ride explores a fascinating region which formed part of Rhode
Island's industrial heartland during the nineteenth century. Lying
midway between Providence and Woonsocket, the area is far
enough from the two cities to be primarily rural, except for the
string of small mill villages nestled along the Blackstone River. Between the villages, you'll ascend onto ridges and then drop down to
the riverbank, where in several places you can see traces of the
150-year-old Blackstone Canal. A scenic highlight of the ride is a
circuit of Lincoln Woods State Park, which has recently been refur-
bished into a recreational showpiece.

Lincoln, an attractive suburban community on the south bank
of the Blackstone, is the starting point of the ride. You pass the
white quarries of the Conklin Limestone Company, a unique geo-
logical feature in the state, before turning onto Great Road, a great
road for biking. Several handsome old buildings have given this
road the status of a State Historic District. As you ascend onto a
ridge with fine views, you'll see the Mowry Tavern, a long wide-
porched building dating from 1686. A long downhill run brings you
past horse farms, weathered barns, and gracious stone houses up
to the entrance to Lincoln Woods State Park.

After a loop around the park, just as you took in Ride 7, head
north on Route 126, paralleling the river. Turn onto a side road and
cross the Blackstone River and the remains of the Blackstone Canal, which runs parallel to it. The canal, which connected Providence with Worcester, was opened in 1828. It closed twenty years
later, unable to compete with the railroad, which could more

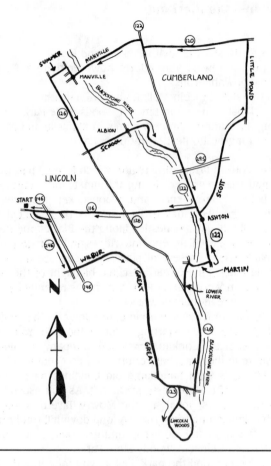

How to get there: From Route 146, exit south onto
Route 116. The mall is just ahead on right at traffic light.
By bike from Providence, head north on Charles Street.
Cross Mineral Spring Avenue (Route 15) and continue for
about 3 miles to second traffic light (Route 123). Turn left
for about 3.5 miles to end (Route 116). Turn right, and
mall is just ahead on left.

Directions for the ride: 24 miles

- Left out of parking lot on Route 116. The entrance ramp to Route 146 is just ahead on your right.
- Bear right for 0.2 mile to Route 246, which bears right just before Route 146.
- Bear right for 0.6 mile to crossroads. Go left on Wilbur Road for 2.5 miles to end (Route 123).
- Left for a half mile to entrance to Lincoln Woods.
- Right for 1.1 miles to fork where main road bears left and smaller dead-end road bears right (sign may point right to picnic areas 29 to 42).
- Bear left. Just ahead curve left, staying on park road (Olney Pond on left). Go a half-mile to fork and bear right on main road for 1.2 miles to end, at stop sign.
- Right for 0.7 mile to end (Route 123, where you entered the park).
- Right for 0.2 mile to fork (traffic light). Eleazar Arnold House on left just before light.
- Bear slightly left for 0.2 mile to another light.
- Left on Route 126 for 1.7 miles to Lower River Road (unmarked), which bears right as you start to climb steep hill. Bear right for 0.3 mile to crossroads at bottom of hill. (Mill village of Quinnville is straight ahead, with Blackstone Canal alongside road.)
- Hairpin right turn at crossroads for 0.6 mile to end (Route 122).
- Left for 0.8 mile to Scott Road, just before traffic light. Short ride goes straight and then left at light. **Caution:** Route 122 is very busy.
- Right for 3.4 miles to end (Route 120, Nate Whipple Highway).
- Left for 2.3 miles to end (Route 122). Jog right and immediately left at traffic light for 0.7 mile to another light at bottom of big hill.
- Right for 0.1 mile to Summer Street, the second left. Take it 0.3 mile to end (Route 126).
- Left for 1.5 miles to crossroads at top of hill.
- Left on School Street for 0.6 mile to crossroads (yellow blinker in middle).
- Straight for 0.9 mile to end (merge into Route 122). (**Caution:** Blinker is yellow for all four roads, so watch for cross traffic.) Just past blinker is steep curving downhill with railroad tracks at bottom.

- Bear right for 0.8 mile to Route 116 on right.
- Right for 2.3 miles to mall entrance on right, at traffic light. Spectacular view from left side of bridge over Blackstone River at beginning of this section.

Directions for the ride: 13 miles

- Follow first 12 directions of long ride to Scott Road.
- Straight for 100 yards, and left at traffic light on Route 116. Go 2.3 miles to mall entrance on right, at traffic light. Spectacular view from left side of bridge over Blackstone River at beginning of this section.

quickly carry much larger payloads. A 19-mile linear historical park along the river, which will include a bikeway, is in the planning stages.

After crossing the river into Cumberland, follow Route 122 through the classic mill village of Ashton, which has not changed much since the Industrial Revolution. On your left are orderly rows of identical brick three-story houses and the sprawling brick mill on the riverbank; on your right is the impressive, Gothic-style Saint Joseph's Church standing guard over the village. If you're taking the short ride, take Route 116 back to Lincoln Mall.

Now head away from the river for several miles through woods and small farms, and a glimpse of unspoiled Sneech Pond. A screaming downhill run—one of the longest and steepest in the state—brings you back into the valley. The river spills over an attractive dam as you cross the bridge into Manville, the largest of the mill towns on the ride. Here brick rowhouses and three- and four-story wooden tenements with wide front porches cling to the steep hillside back from the river. Two miles ahead descend into Albion, another mill village with a fascinating variety of architecture. Along the river stretches another brick fortress of a mill, this one belonging to American Tourister. Cross briefly into Cumberland and then back to Lincoln over the high bridge on Route 116.

9. Chepachet—Scituate—Foster—East Killingly

Number of miles: 15 (31 with Foster-East Killingly extension)
Terrain: Challenging; in other words, hilly.
Start: Park and Shop supermarket, Route 44, Chepachet.
Food: Country store at corner of Routes 94 and 101. Snack bar
   in Chepachet, at end. Burger King and McDonald's, corner of
   Routes 44 and 5, eight miles east of starting point.

This ride explores the wooded hills and unspoiled ponds of western
Rhode Island, about 20 miles west of Providence. The terrain is
hilly, but the effort expended in climbing will be rewarded by some
exciting downhill runs, including one of the longest in the state on
the 31-mile ride. Because the region is thinly populated, you will
not encounter much traffic. The only busy road, Route 101, has a
safe and smooth shoulder.

From the ride's starting point in Chepachet, head south on
Route 102, which climbs gradually through woodland to the top of
Chopmist Hill, one of the highest points in the state, with an elevation of 730 feet. The short ride turns west on Route 101 and
plunges down a spectacular descent with a sweeping view, only to
climb again up Pray Hill, which you'll agree is appropriately named.
Some maps spell it Prey, also appropriate. The return trip to Chepachet is nearly all downhill on rural lanes winding through dense
forest and occasional patches of pasture. Shortly before the end is
the Smith and Sayles Reservoir on Chestnut Hill Road.

The long ride continues south on Route 102 along the crest of
Chopmist Hill. You'll pass the gracious Chopmist Hill Inn, known for
its fine restaurant. Just ahead, revel in one of the state's longest
downhills, a steady mile-long descent to the western edge of the
Scituate Reservoir, the largest lake in Rhode Island. The picnic area
at the bottom of the hill is a good spot for a breather; it has a pump
where you can refill your water bottle with pure spring water. You
can visit a lovely, unspoiled falls a half mile off the route by turning
right onto Ponagansett Road 0.4 mile after the picnic area.

A tough climb out of the watershed will bring you into the
small village of Clayville. Now angle northwest through Foster, a

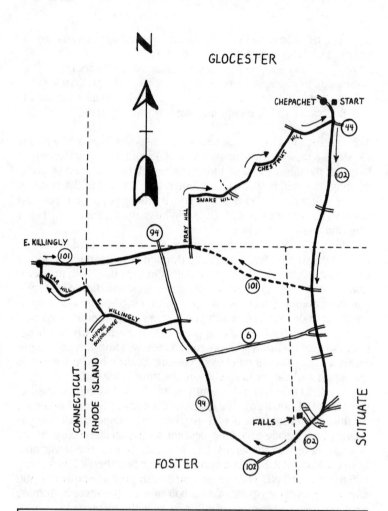

How to get there: From Route 295, exit west onto Route 44 and go about 9 miles to parking lot on right, at corner of Douglas Hook Road.

Directions for the ride: 31 miles

- Left out of parking lot on Route 44 for 0.3 mile to fork.
- Bear right on Route 102 for 4.6 miles to second traffic light (Route 101). Here the short ride turns right.
- Straight for 5.8 miles to fork where Route 102 bears left and Route 94 bears right, about a mile beyond Clayville.
- Bear right for 3.9 miles to wide crossroads (Route 6).
- Straight for 1.3 miles to crossroads (East Killingly Road). Go left for 1.6 miles to fork.
- Bear right for 0.9 mile to another fork and bear left on the main road, Bear Hill Road, for 1.7 miles to end (merge right at stop sign, in East Killingly).
- Bear right for 0.1 mile to end (Route 101).
- Right for 3.2 miles to traffic light (Route 94). Go straight for 1.1 miles to crossroads at top of hill. (Pray Hill Road on left.)
- Left on Pray Hill Road for 2.3 miles to fork.
- Bear left on Chestnut Hill Road for 0.9 mile to a wide intersection where the main road curves left and a smaller road goes straight. Stay on main road for 2.1 miles to end.
- Right (still Chestnut Hill Road) for 1 mile to end (Route 44).
- Left for 0.3 mile to parking lot on right.

Directions for the ride: 15 miles

- Follow first 2 directions of long ride, to Route 101.
- Right for 3.4 miles to crossroads at top of hill (Pray Hill Road on right).
- Right for 2.3 miles to fork.
- Follow last 3 directions of long ride.

completely rural town along the Connecticut border. In the tiny center of town, 100 yards to the left of Route 94 about two miles beyond Clayville, is the country's oldest town hall (built in 1796) which is still in use. Continue on to East Killingly Road, a rural byway which brings you to the Connecticut border, past the graceful North Foster Baptist Church and the Maple Glen Inn, a good restaurant.

A narrow road takes you into Connecticut, descending steeply into the mill village of East Killingly. Just before the village you'll parallel a chain of three small millponds, with two dams on your left. The second dam is across from the old brick and stone mill; you'll miss it unless you look for it. Route 101 takes you out of town and on a steep climb to the Rhode Island line. A more gradual ascent leads to the summit of Jerimoth Hill, the highest point in Rhode Island, with an elevation of 812 feet. Descend slowly for a half mile, passing the state's largest sawmill, and climb sharply once more to the top of Pray Hill, to rejoin the short ride.

10. Scituate Spins, 1 and 2

Number of miles: 16 (Scituate Spin 1) or 18 (Scituate Spin 2)
Terrain: Rolling with one long hill.
Start: North Scituate Town Common, Route 116, just south of
  Route 6.
Food: Knight Farms, corner of Snake Hill Road and Route 116.
  Grocery, corner of Snake Hill Road and Sawmill Road. Snack
  bars in North Scituate, at end. Judith Helene's, on Danielson
  Pike, is excellent.

The town of Scituate, ten to fifteen miles west of Providence, provides superb bicycling on a network of winding, wooded roads with
very little traffic. The town is dominated by the state's largest lake,
the Scituate Reservoir, which you can bike around on Ride 13. Here
are a pair of rides that loop through the northern half of the town,
leading you along back roads through boulder-strewn forests,
across the reservoir's northern arm, and past several apple orchards. Although the two rides are in the same area, there is almost
no overlap between them.

Both rides begin in North Scituate, the largest village in the
town of Scituate. It is an attractive community of old homes, with a
handsome brick library and a graceful white church opposite the
Common. Behind the Common is an elegant white apartment
building with tall columns which was formerly the Watchman Institute. In early October, North Scituate comes alive as the site of
Rhode Island's second largest art festival.

For the first ride, head south out of town on Route 116, riding
through the dense evergreens banking the northern arm of the reservoir. Turn west on Route 14, and enjoy the long descent to the
causeway that curves across the northern arm. Now you must
tackle the toughest climb of the ride as you head north on Trimtown Road, which ascends gradually past homes nestled in the
woods.

You'll be justly rewarded for the climb when you turn onto Central Pike, a freshly repaved road that drops steeply back into the
watershed. At the end of the road is the headquarters of the State

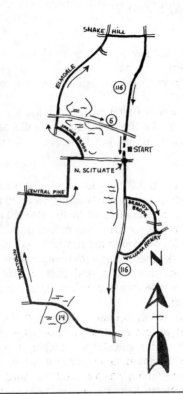

How to get there: From Route 295, exit west on Route 6 for about 3.5 miles to Route 116. Turn left for 0.2 miles to parking lot on left, across from church. By bike from Providence, head west from Olneyville Square on Plainfield Street. Go 0.8 mile to Sunset Avenue on right, opposite Lowell Avenue. Bear right for 0.3 mile to fork. Bear left uphill for 1.7 miles to traffic light (Route 5). Straight for 2.5 miles to fork (Bishop Road bears right). Bear right for 1.2 miles to fork (Pine Hill Road bears left). Bear left for 1.2 miles to end (Danielson Pike). Left for 0.2 mile to Route 116. Right for 0.2 mile to parking lot on right opposite church.

Directions for the ride: 16 miles (Scituate Spin 1)

- Left out of parking lot on Route 116 for 0.2 mile to traffic light (Danielson Pike).
- Straight for 0.6 mile to Brandy Brook Road. Go left for 0.9 mile to crossroads (Central Pike).
- Straight for 0.1 mile to end (merge left).
- Sharp right on William Henry Road for 1.2 miles to end (Route 116).
- Left for 1.5 miles to crossroads (Route 14).
- Right for 2.1 miles to Trimtown Road on right, at top of hill.
- Right for 2 miles to crossroads (Central Pike).
- Right for 1.5 miles to end (Danielson Pike). (**Caution:** Road curves 90 degrees left at bottom of big hill.)
- Right for one quarter mile to Spring Brook Road (sign says Scituate Facility). Go left for 0.6 mile to end (Elmdale Road).
- Right for 0.1 mile to Route 6.
- Straight for 1.8 miles to where a wider road turns right and a smaller road bears slightly left. Bear left (still Elmdale Road) for 0.6 mile to crossroads and stop sign (Snake Hill Road).
- Right for a half mile to crossroads. Take Route 116 on right for 1.9 miles to traffic light (Route 6).
- Straight for 0.2 mile to parking lot on left.

Directions for the ride: 18 miles (Scituate Spin 2)

- Right out of parking lot on Route 116 for 0.2 mile to traffic light (Route 6).
- Straight for 0.4 mile to Peeptoad Road.
- Left for 1.4 miles to end (Elmdale Road).
- Right for 0.7 mile to where a wider road turns right and a smaller road bears slightly left. Bear left (still Elmdale Road) for a half mile to crossroads and stop sign (Snake Hill Road).
- Left for 1.1 miles to crossroads and blinking light.
- Straight for 0.8 mile to fork. **Caution:** Bumpy downhill. Take it easy.
- Bear left downhill on Sandy Brook Road for 2.2 miles to end (Rocky Hill Road).
- Right for 0.7 mile to where Gleaner Chapel Road turns left and main road bears right.

- Bear right for 1.4 miles to where Bungy Road (unmarked) turns right and main road bears left. Tough hill at beginning.
- Bear left for one mile to end (Route 101).
- Right for 0.6 mile to traffic light (Route 102).
- Left for 1.1 mile to traffic light (Route 6). Just ahead is another light. Straight for 1.1 miles to crossroads (Central Pike, unmarked).
- Left for 1.8 miles to diagonal crossroads and stop sign at bottom of hill (Rockland Road). Straight for 1.5 miles to end (Danielson Pike). **Caution:** Road curves 90 degrees left at bottom of big hill.
- Right for one mile to traffic light (Route 116), in North Scituate.
- Left for 0.2 mile to parking lot on right.

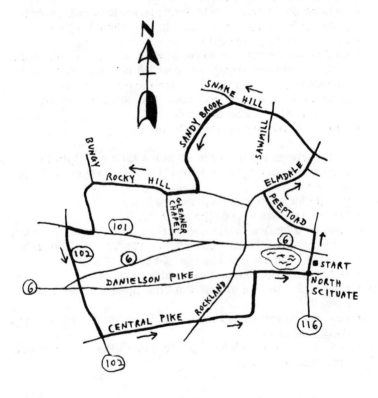

Police. Turn onto Spring Brook Road, a narrow lane paralleling the reservoir near its most northerly point.

Spring Brook Road leads into Elmdale Road, an idyllic byway bobbing up and down small rises through dense, boulder-dotted woodland. You pass tiny Peeptoad Pond on your left, and suddenly enter orchard country. The area north and west of here is the prime apple-growing region of Rhode Island, with orderly rows of apple trees covering the hillsides. Many of the orchards, like Knight Farms just up the road, have fruit and cider stands that are good refreshment stops for the cyclist. Across the road, incongruous among the orchards, is an underground data storage area. Now turn south on Route 116 to finish the ride, passing a couple more orchards and Moswansicut Pond, set back from the road on the left.

The second ride heads northwest out of town on Peeptoad Road, a winding lane that seems to have been custom-designed for the bicyclist. You will pass the observatory of the Skyscrapers, an amateur astronomy club. Sandy Brook Road, another narrow country lane, snakes past two small ponds and a little dam. The one tough climb of the ride, on Rocky Hill Road, brings you onto Chopmist Hill, a long, high ridge. A fire tower and a pair of radio towers stand at the highest point. After a flat run along the ridge on Route 102, your reward comes on Central Pike, a smooth, lightly-traveled road that runs primarily downhill for several miles past farms, weathered barns, and secluded country homes bordered by stone walls. Just before the end, pedal along the northern portion of the Scituate Reservoir.

11. Providence East Side Ride

Number of miles: 10
Terrain: Rolling, with several short hills and one tough one.
Start: IGA Supermarket, corner of Pitman Street and Butler
Avenue, on the East Side of Providence.
Food: Several snack bars on Thayer Street, two blocks off the
route near Brown University.

This is one of only three rides in the book that is urban rather than
rural. Nine-tenths of Providence is unsuitable for enjoyable biking,
but fortunately there is one section of the city, the East Side, which
is tailor-made for a safe, leisurely two-wheel jaunt.

The East Side, situated between the downtown area and the
Seekonk River, is the wealthiest and the most historic part of the
city. The ride starts off with a run along the river, which twenty
years ago was an open sewer but now is a clean and attractive
waterway. You head inland briefly through a gracious residential
area, passing Butler Hospital, a private psychiatric hospital which
looks like an old graceful college campus.

Just north of the hospital is the rolling, meticulously landscaped
Swan Point Cemetery, where little lanes, dipping up and down
along the bluffs overlooking the river, wind past impressive crypts
and monuments. Here is buried H. P. Lovecraft, America's best-
known author of horror tales since Edgar Allen Poe.

Leaving the cemetery, head south on famed Blackstone Boulevard, the jogging capital of Rhode Island, with its broad grassy center island and impressive homes on both sides. Then head across
the middle of the East Side along Freeman Parkway, one of the
finest streets in Providence, with its large, elegant residences. Just
ahead is the Moses Brown School, an exclusive prep school with a
magnificent old campus. Now cross Thayer Street, the main commercial "strip" for the Brown University community. Here are three
blocks lined with boutiques, bookstores, little restaurants, and the
enduring Avon movie theater. An unlocked bike here has a life ex-
pectancy of about one minute.

You now climb gradually to the crest of College Hill, which

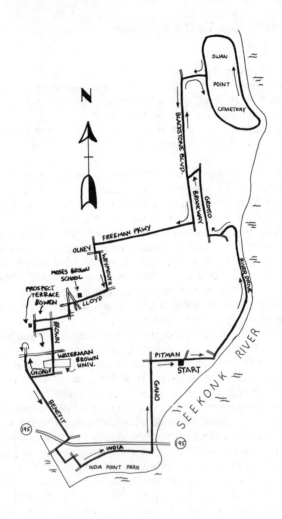

How to get there: From Route 195 (the section east of I-95), take the Gano Street exit. Turn right at end of exit ramp for half mile to Pitman Street, at traffic light. Right for quarter mile to IGA on right.

Directions for the ride

- Right out of parking lot for a quarter mile to small rotary (Seekonk River on right). Pass Richmond Square, formerly an old factory, now a high-tech office park.
- Straight along river for 0.9 mile to end (merge right at top of steep hill on Loring Avenue).
- Bear right for one block to end (Grotto Avenue).
- Right for 0.4 mile to Brookway Road on left, at bottom of hill.
- Left for 0.1 mile to end (Blackstone Boulevard).
- Right for 0.6 mile to entrance to Swan Point Cemetery on right.
- Bear right into the cemetery, explore it, and leave it at the same place where you entered. (There is only one entrance.)
- Bear left on Blackstone Boulevard for 0.9 mile to Freeman Parkway, after house number 180.
- Right for 0.7 mile to end (Morris Avenue).
- Left for one block to crossroads (Olney Street); go left for 100 yards to first right (Weymouth Street).
- Right for 0.2 mile to end (Lloyd Avenue).
- Right for 0.3 mile to second crossroads (Thayer Street). Moses Brown School is on right at top of hill. **Caution:** First crossroads is very busy.
- Left for one block to crossroads (Bowen Street); go right for 0.3 mile to end (Congdon Street).
- Left for one block to first left (Cushing Street). Prospect Terrace is on right.
- Left for 0.2 mile to second crossroads (Brown Street).
- Right for 0.2 mile to end (Waterman Street).
- Straight through arch into main quadrangle of Brown University. Go 0.1 mile to first street (George Street.) (**Caution:** Curb at George Street.)
- Right for 0.2 mile to end at Benefit Street. (**Caution:** Steep downhill.)
- Right for two blocks to traffic light (Waterman Street). First Baptist Church is on left just past light.
- Make a U-turn. Go south on Benefit Street for 0.6 mile to traffic light at end.
- Right for 100 yards to another light, immediately after going under Route 195.

- Left on South Main Street for 0.2 mile to end (India Street), at waterfront. Hurricane barrier on right. A planned condominium complex may displace this part of India Street. If this occurs, turn left after one block on Tockwotton Street, go 0.2 mile to end (India Street), and left along waterfront.
- Left for a half mile to Gano Street on left. Turn left for 0.6 mile to Pitman Street, at traffic light. (**Caution:** Gano Street is busy. Watch for traffic at Route 195 entrance and exit ramps.)
- Right for a quarter mile to parking lot on right.

drops steeply toward the downtown area. Perched on the brow of the hill is Prospect Terrace, a grassy overlook with a superb view of the city. On the grounds is a large statue of Roger Williams, who is buried here.

A few blocks ahead, cross the central quadrangle of Brown University, containing its oldest building, University Hall, built in 1770. A block from the campus is historic Benefit Street, which runs along the side of College Hill one block up from the downtown area. In quick succession, you pass an impressive cluster of historic landmarks, beginning with the flawlessly preserved First Baptist Church, built in 1775, then the Museum of Art of the Rhode Island School of Design, one of the country's finest small museums. Across the street is the Providence Athenaeum, a private library open to visitors, built in 1838 in Greek Revival style. Next is the imposing, brick Superior Courthouse, opposite Athenaeum Row, a graceful brick apartment house built in 1856. Immediately beyond the Courthouse is the Stephen Hopkins House (1707 with 1743 addition), home of the ten-time governor of Rhode Island and signer of the Declaration of Independence.

Continuing south on Benefit Street, pass the graceful First Unitarian Church (1816), which contains the largest bell cast by Paul Revere, and the palatial John Brown House (1786), which John Quincy Adams described as "the most magnificent and elegant private mansion that I have ever seen on this continent." After amassing a fortune as a China Trade merchant, slave trader, and privateer, John Brown wanted to build a mansion that would awe and inspire his visitors. It is now the headquarters of the Rhode Island Historical Society and open to the public.

Just past the foot of Benefit Street you go along the southern edge of the East Side, fronting on Providence Harbor. This is an area where old warehouses and factories are being replaced by, or recycled into, luxury condominiums. Cross the Fox Point Hurricane Barrier, a series of gates that can be closed to prevent storm-driven water from flooding the city as it did during the terrible hurricanes of 1938 and 1954. Just ahead is the dock for the ferry to Newport and Block Island, a superb four-hour trip. The rest of the waterfront consists of India Point Park.

The last mile of the ride goes through a predominantly Portuguese neighborhood of well-kept, closely spaced dwellings.

12. Scituate—Foster

Number of miles: 19 (33 with Connecticut border extension, or
    28 with short cut)
Terrain: Rolling, with two difficult climbs. To reward your efforts,
    however, finish with one of the best downhill runs in the
    state.
Start: Picnic area at junction of Route 102, Route 14, and
    Rockland Road, known as Crazy Corners, in Scituate.
Food: Country store and small restaurant on Route 6.

Challenging but very scenic, this ride takes you through rural
Rhode Island at its finest. Foster, an unspoiled country town hugging the Connecticut border twenty miles west of Providence, is a
magnificent bicycling area of winding roller-coaster roads, passing
small farms edged by stone walls, with old weathered barns.

The ride begins in Scituate at the western edge of the Scituate
Reservoir. (A half mile from the start, just off the route, you can visit
a beautiful falls along the small stream connecting the Barden and
Scituate reservoirs.) You parallel the western arm of the reservoir
on Route 12, a quiet, well-paved road. After a couple of miles turn
west onto Old Plainfield Pike, which climbs gradually with an occasional steep pitch. Originally this road continued farther east across
land which is now beneath the reservoir.

When the route turns north onto Howard Hill Road, there is a
gentle downhill run drifting past sturdy farmhouses, a tiny cemetery, and pastures dotted with cows and horses. You pass through
Foster Center, whose Town House is the nation's oldest town hall in
continuous use. You turn east onto Central Pike to begin the most
exciting portion of the ride. A screaming downhill run on the
freshly-repaved road zips you to the small bridge across the Barden
Reservoir; then you pay the price on a sweat-producing grind up to
Route 102. But once again you'll be rewarded with a long, steady
downgrade back to your starting point, guaranteed to leave you in
good spirits.

The long ride heads farther west, inching toward the Connecticut state line on more peaceful back roads. On Johnson Road you

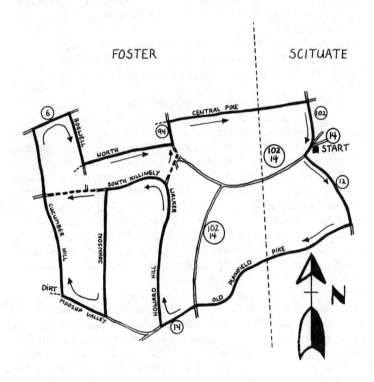

FOSTER

SCITUATE

6

BOSWELL

CENTRAL PIKE

94

102

14
START

102
14

12

NORTH

SOUTH KILLINGLY

WALKER

CUCUMBER HILL

JOHNSON

HOWARD HILL

102
14

DIRT

MOOSUP VALLEY

OLD PLAINFIELD PIKE

14

N

How to get there: From Route 295, exit west on Route 14. Picnic area is 9 miles ahead on right.

Directions for the ride: 33 or 28 miles

(Before you leave, fill your water bottle from the pump between Route 102 and Rockland Road.)

- Head south (downhill) on Route 102 for 0.6 mile to Route 12 on left. (To visit falls, turn right after 0.4 mile on Ponagansett Road for a half mile. Waterfall is on left just past crossroads.)
- Left for 2.5 miles to Old Plainfield Pike on right.
- Right for 4.3 miles to Route 102. Cross Route 102 onto Route 14. Go 1.1 miles to Howard Hill Road on right.
- Right for 3.8 miles to stop sign where South Killingly Road turns left and Walker Road bears right. (Sign may point left to Foster Country Club.) Here the short ride bears right.
- Left for 1.4 miles to Johnson Road on left, while going downhill. (You can shorten the ride to 28 miles by staying straight on South Killingly Road for 1.9 miles to crossroads, Cucumber Hill Road. Right for 1.6 miles to Route 6.)
- Left on Johnson Road for 3.1 miles to end (Moosup Valley Road).
- Right for 5.7 miles to end (Route 6). Go right for 1.1 miles to Boswell Trail.
- Right for 1.7 miles to crossroads (North Road). Dirt road on right.
- Left for 2.3 miles to end (Route 94).
- Left for 0.8 mile to crossroads (Central Pike). Dirt road on left.
- Right for 3.6 miles to crossroads at top of hill (Route 102). **Caution:** Potholes and gravel on bridge at bottom of big hill.
- Right for 1.3 miles to picnic area on left.

Directions for the ride: 19 miles

- Follow first four directions of long ride to Walker Road on right.
- Bear right for a half mile to another fork, in Foster Center (note old bell-towered schoolhouse, now a library, on right). Bear left for 100 yards to end (Route 94).
- Left for 1.1 miles to crossroads (Central Pike). Dirt road on left.
- Follow last two directions of long ride.

pass the Dyer Woods Nudist Camp, the only one in the state, and the tidy fairways of the Foster Country Club. The terrain levels out for the remainder of the longer loop. Cucumber Hill Road ascends gradually and then descends past broad farms. On Route 6, the only busy road on the ride, you can stop for a breather at a small restaurant or grocery store. After several more miles along narrow wooded roads, rejoin the short ride for the Central Pike portion of the ride.

13. Scituate Reservoir

Number of miles: 23 (9 omitting loop around reservoir)
Terrain: Hilly.
Start: North Scituate Town Common, Route 116, just south of
  Route 6.
Food: Snack bar at Hazard Indian Rock Orchard, a quarter mile
  off Route 12 on Burnt Hill Road. Pizza at corner of Routes 6
  and 116, 0.2 mile north of starting point.

This is a hilly but beautiful ride around Rhode Island's largest lake.
The Scituate Reservoir is one of the state's finest natural resources,
with its shoreline completely undeveloped and surrounded by a
broad belt of pine trees. The water is very pure, enabling Providence to have one of the highest quality water supplies in the East
for a city of its size. The dam on Route 12, along the southeastern
shore, and the causeway on Route 14 across the center of the
reservoir, provide two of the most scenic runs in the state.

As with Ride 10, the attractive village of North Scituate, located
at the northern tip of the reservoir, makes a nice beginning for this
ride. Start by heading south through the thick evergreens that completely encircle the lake. You can catch glimpses of the water
through the trees on your right. Soon you turn away from the water
as you climb onto a ridge along Central Pike and Peck Hill Road.
There's a fine view on your right across a stretch of open farmland.
Just ahead, turn west on Route 14, heading back toward the reservoir and the end of the short ride.

To begin the fourteen-mile loop around the main part of the
lake, cross Route 116, and soon your bike sprouts wings on a long,
steady descent to the half-mile-long causeway that spans the
northern arm. The road continues for about three miles to the
western edge of the reservoir, climbing and descending several
steep grades. On this stretch you pass two well-manicured horse
paddocks on the left, and a massive maple tree, surrounded by a
small plot of grass, on the right. At the junction of Routes 14 and
102 there's a picnic area with a pump where you can refill your
water bottle. (Turn right on Ponagansett Road for a half mile if you

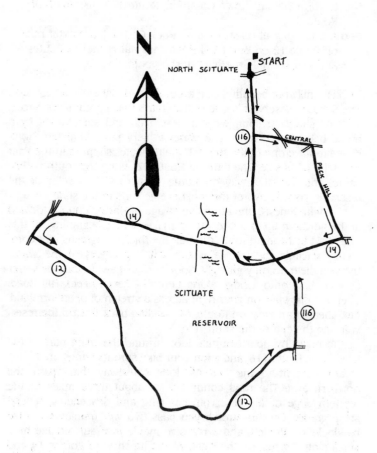

START

NORTH SCITUATE

N

(116)

CENTRAL

PECK HILL

(14)

(14)

(12)

SCITUATE

RESERVOIR

(116)

(12)

How to get there: Same as Ride 10.

Directions for the ride: 23 miles

- Left out of parking lot for 0.2 mile to traffic light (Danielson Pike).
- Straight for one mile to second left (Central Pike).
- Left for 0.6 mile to crossroads, then straight for 0.3 mile to Peck Hill Road.
- Turn right for 1.8 mile to end (Route 14). Don't turn very sharp right on William Henry Road.
- Right for 1.4 miles to crossroads (Route 116). Here the short ride turns right.
- Straight for 4.5 miles to where you merge left into Route 102.
- Bear left for 0.6 mile to Route 12 on left. (To see falls, turn right after 0.4 mile to Ponagansett Road on right. Go a half mile to falls on left.)
- Left on Route 12 for 7.2 miles to crossroads (Route 116). To visit Hazard Indian Rock Orchard, turn sharp right after 5 miles on Burnt Hill Road. Go a quarter mile to orchard on right.
- Left on Route 116 for 2 miles to crossroads (Route 14).
- Straight for 3.3 miles to traffic light (Danielson Pike).
- Straight for 0.2 mile to parking lot on right.

Directions for the ride: 9 miles

- Follow first 5 directions of long ride to junction of Routes 14 and 116.
- Right for 3.3 miles to traffic light (Danielson Pike).
- Straight for 0.2 mile to parking lot on right.

want to visit some beautiful, unspoiled falls.)

Now turn east on Route 12, a silk-smooth road that hugs the shore for a mile and then gradually climbs away from the water. At the top, you'll enjoy the best downhill run of the ride, an exhilarating descent which becomes steadily steeper. At the top of the next hill turn into Hazard Indian Rock Orchards, a great snack stop with fresh cider and homemade pie. You descend again, and as you swing around a curve you suddenly see the whole reservoir before you, with the road stretching arrow-straight along the top of Gainer Memorial Dam, nearly a mile long. Just beyond the dam turn north on Route 116, which will bring you back to North Scituate. The road diverges from the water through dense woodland for several miles, and returns to the shore just before the town.

14. Western Cranston

Number of miles: 18 (29 with Scituate Reservoir extension)
Terrain: Rolling. The long ride is hilly.
Start: Stop and Shop, junction of Routes 5 and 12, Cranston.
Food: Snack bar at Hazard Indian Rock Orchard, a quarter mile
      off Route 12 on Burnt Hill Road. Grocery at corner of Route
      14 and Pippin Orchard Road. Farm stand and cider mill on
      Pippin Orchard Road.

This ride will come to many as a pleasant surprise. When you think of Cranston, you probably picture the congested neighborhoods and commercial arteries just south of Providence. But the western third of the city, beyond Route 295, is amazingly rural, with large farms that have not yet been sold to developers. Pedalling along Hope and Seven Mile Roads, you would think you were in Iowa rather than less than ten miles from downtown Providence.

You start the ride by heading south on Phenix Avenue, a wide, smooth road that passes the extensive grounds of Cranston West High School and a gravel plant. Soon you bear off onto less-traveled roads and cross a picturesque brook cascading down a hillside past the ruins of a small mill. Hope Road ascends gradually through open farmland, and if you look back over your left shoulder, you will enjoy the fine views.

After a couple of miles descend to the valley of the Pawtuxet River along a fast, smooth downhill run. Parallel the river, passing several brick and stone mills from the turn of the century as you nick the northeast corner of Coventry. Then swing northward, back into farmland along Seven Mile Road, a delight for bicycling. As you ascend gradually onto a ridge, extensive views unfold to the west.

You'll pass an attractive white church, several small cemeteries, and the Curran Upper Reservoir before turning west onto Route 12. As you start downhill, a panoramic view of the Scituate Reservoir suddenly greets you. The descent into the watershed is a screamer that unfortunately ends abruptly with a stop sign at the bottom. Here the two rides diverge. The rest of the short ride continues

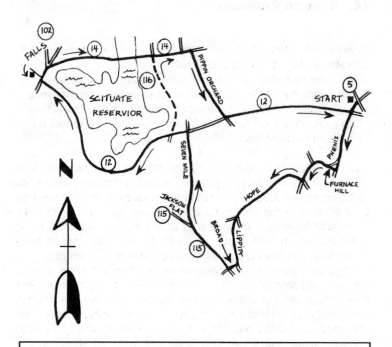

How to get there: From the north, head south on I-95 to Route 10 North, take first exit, Reservoir Avenue. Go south 0.6 mile to Park Avenue (Route 12). Right for about 2 miles to parking lot on right just past Atwood Avenue (Route 5). From the south, head north on I-95 to Route 37 West. Go a half mile to end (Route 51). Right for about 2 miles to parking lot on left, just past traffic light. From the northwest, head south on Route 295 to Route 14. Turn left (east) for 15 miles to Route 5. Right for 1.3 miles to parking lot on right, just before Route 12. By bike from Providence, head southwest out of Olneyville Square on Pocasset Avenue. Go about 2 miles to Cranston Street, at traffic light. Right for 0.8 mile to Park Avenue, at traffic light. Right for a half mile to parking lot on right, just past Atwood Avenue (Route 5).

Directions for the ride: 29 miles

- Right out of parking lot on Route 12 for 0.2 mile to traffic light (Route 12 on right).
- Straight on Phenix Avenue for 1.5 miles to where the main road curves left and a smaller road goes straight up a sharp hill.
- Curve left for 0.2 mile to Furnace Hill Road, right for 0.1 mile to end, and left for 0.6 mile to fork (Olney Arnold Road bears right).
- Bear left for 0.4 mile to crossroads (Hope Road bears right).
- Bear right for 2.3 miles to crossroads (Hope Road on right again).
- Straight on Lippitt Avenue for 0.9 mile to Broad Street, which bears right just before bottom of hill.
- Bear right for 0.2 mile to crossroads (Route 115).
- Right for one mile to where Route 115 (Jackson Flat Road) bears left and Seven Mile Road goes straight. Go straight for 2.2 miles to Route 12.
- Left for one mile to crossroads (Route 116). (**Caution:** Stop sign at bottom of steep hill.) Here the short ride turns right.
- Straight for 7.2 miles to end (Routes 102 and 14). To visit Indian Rock Orchards (food), bear left for a quarter mile at top of hill after dam on Burnt Hill Road.
- Right for 0.6 mile to three-way fork (Route 14 bears right). To visit falls, turn left after 0.2 mile on Ponagansett Road and go a half mile. Falls are on left just past crossroads.
- Bear right on Route 14 for 4.5 miles to crossroads (Route 116).
- Straight for 1.4 miles to Pippin Orchard Road (snack bar on corner).
- Right for 1.6 miles to crossroads (Route 12).
- Left for 3.2 miles to traffic light (Phenix Avenue).
- Left on Route 12 for 0.2 mile to parking lot on left.

Directions for the ride: 18 miles

- Follow first 9 directions of long ride, to junction of Routes 12 and 116.
- Right for 2 miles to crossroads (Route 14).
- Right for 1.4 miles to Pippin Orchard Road on right (snack bar on corner).
- Follow last 3 directions of long ride.

along roads which are a little busier but still fine for biking, with good shoulders and plenty of room for cars to pass. From Route 116 watch for unspoiled Betty Pond on your right, nestled in the woods. Pippin Orchard Road traverses a ridge where you'll probably have a tailwind to help you along. The last stretch along Route 12 is mostly downhill as you descend from the plateau.

The long ride includes a circle around Scituate Reservoir. The terrain is hilly, but the beauty of the landscape makes the effort worthwhile. The ride rejoins the short ride at the intersection of Routes 116 and 14.

15. East Providence—Riverside

Number of miles: 15
Terrain: Gently rolling, with two hills.
Start: East Providence Cycle, 414 Warren Avenue, East
    Providence.
Food: Numerous snack bars and grocery stores along route.

Here is a tour of the southern half of East Providence, a residential community directly across the uppermost part of Narragansett Bay from Providence. Although the region is suburban, its long frontage on the bay provides pleasant and scenic bicycling.

The ride starts about a mile inland from the Providence River, which is actually the relatively narrow northern arm of Narragansett Bay. Head inland briefly through Kent Heights, a pleasant residential area on a high ridge overlooking the rest of East Providence, passing the big red-and-white water tower. A mile ahead, bike past a forest of gasoline and oil tanks at a refinery of the Mobil Oil Corporation. The oil arrives by tanker at the dock two miles away, and is pumped through an above-ground pipeline to the refinery.

Beyond the refinery, head south and west through Riverside, the residential southern quarter of East Providence. Just before you come to the bay, you'll see a large, modern apartment complex on your left, built on the former grounds of Crescent Park, one of New England's leading amusement parks during the early 1900s. Next to the apartments is a round, gaily painted building containing a masterpiece of folk art, an ornately carved 62-horse carousel constructed in 1895 by Charles Looff, a noted woodcarver. When the park went out of business in 1975, the land reverted to the city, which sold it several years later to the developer who built the apartments. An enraged citizenry, fearful that the carousel would be demolished, sued to have it brought back under city ownership, and recently won their suit. The carousel is still in operating condition and is open during the summer.

Now loop around residential Bullocks Point, a narrow peninsula forming the southern tip of East Providence, and continue on to Sabin Point, a small park surrounded by the bay on three sides. A

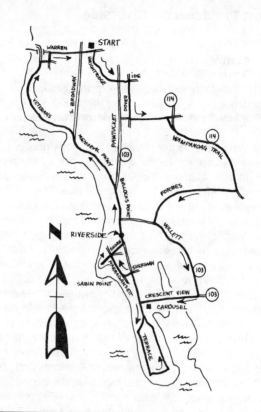

How to get there: From I-95, head east on Route 195 to exit 6 (sign says Broadway). Turn right, and the shop is the first building on your right. From the east on Route 195, take exit 6 (sign says East Providence). Turn left, go to traffic light at Warren Avenue; turn left for 0.2 mile to store on left. By bike from Providence, head east on Waterman Street, cross bridge over Seekonk River, and take first exit. Just ahead road curves 90 degrees left. Take second right on Walnut Street for 0.6 mile to end (Warren Avenue), shortly after you cross Taunton Avenue. Left for 0.8 mile to shore on left.

Directions for the ride

- Left on Warren Avenue for 0.1 mile to second right (Brightridge Avenue). Take it for 0.6 mile to end (Pawtucket Avenue).
- Jog left and immediatly right on Ide Avenue for one block to crossroads (Dover Avenue).
- Right for a half mile to crossroads and stop sign (Wampanoag Trail).
- Left for a half mile to Route 114 (sign says Barrington, Bristol).
- Right for 1.8 miles to Forbes Street, after access road to Mobil refinery.
- Right for 1.4 miles to end (Willett Avenue).
- Left for 1.3 miles to end (Crescent View Avenue; sign says Riverside).
- Right for 0.7 mile to end (Bullocks Point Avenue). Carousel on left at corner. (After a quarter mile you'll cross the East Bay Bike Path, which leads about three miles on your left to Barrington and, when completed, will go to Bristol). Left on Bullocks Point Avenue for 0.2 mile to fork.
- Bear right on Terrace Avenue. After 0.7 mile, road turns 90 degrees left, then 90 degrees left again just ahead. Continue for 1.3 miles to small crossroads (Sherman Street); house number 493 on left corner.
- Left for 0.1 mile to end (Narragansett Avenue).
- Right for 0.3 mile to crossroads and stop sign (Shore Road).
- Left for 0.2 mile to end, at Sabin Point Park.
- Make a U-turn and go 0.2 mile to fork (North Street bears right).
- Continue straight for a quarter mile to end (Bullocks Point Avenue).
- Left for 1.6 miles to fork, at traffic light (Route 103 bears right). (**Caution:** This stretch is very busy.)
- Go straight (don't bear right) at fork onto Veterans Memorial Parkway. (**Caution:** It's safest to walk the intersection because traffic in the right lane of Bullocks Point Avenue is forced to bear right at the fork.) Go 0.8 mile to fork at bottom of hill (South Broadway bears right).
- Bear left for 1.5 miles to road on right at bottom of hill (sign says to Warren Avenue).
- Right for one short block to crossroads (Burgess Avenue).
- Left for one block to end (Warren Avenue).
- Right for 0.8 mile to store on left, shortly after the traffic light at Broadway.

little farther on is the Mobil dock, with more storage tanks. Turn left just past Willett Avenue into the parking lot of the Stone Gate Condominiums, to get a view of an old, picturesque lighthouse perched on a tiny island a few hundred feet offshore.

Proceed on to Veterans Memorial Parkway, a smooth road with a good shoulder which starts off by going down a long, gentle hill. This is one of the nicest biking runs in the metropolitan Providence area. On your left is Squantum Woods, a small state park which works its way down to the bay between more storage tanks, a hospital for handicapped children, an exclusive private club, and an old railroad embankment. At the bottom of the hill is Watchemoket Cove, a small inlet. Just ahead you ascend onto a low ridge with dramatic views of downtown Providence across the river. At the end of the Parkway, it's only a mile back to the starting point.

16. Coventry—West Greenwich

Number of miles: 16 (28 with West Greenwich extension)
Terrain: Rolling, with some gradual hills. The long ride is hilly, with two real monsters.
Start: Burger King, Route 3, Coventry.
Food: Genuine, old-fashioned country store in Summit. Burger King at end, and McDonald's across the road.

This ride is a tour of the sparsely populated countryside that extends west toward the Connecticut border from the dead center of the state. It begins in Coventry, a long, rectangular town that extends from the Connecticut state line to just five miles from Narragansett Bay. This is a town with two sharply contrasting sections. The eastern third is fairly built up, but the western section is completely rural, with only the three tiny villages of Coventry Center, Summit, and Greene tucked away amidst the rocky, wooded landscape.

The starting point lies on the dividing line between these two sections. After a brief stretch on Route 3, you head into woodland when you turn onto Hill Farm Road. Cross a small bridge over the Flat River Reservoir that feeds into the Pawtuxet River. The road climbs gradually onto a forested ridge that drops down to the reservoir on your right. Cross Route 117 in Coventry Center, a small village with a couple of old mills, then ride alongside the Flat River Reservoir, and rejoin Route 117, a wide, well-paved road with a good shoulder and not much traffic.

You proceed on to the village of Summit, containing a few old houses, small church, and marvelous old-fashioned country store hidden on a back road, which used to be part of Route 117. The short ride turns south briefly past rich farmland and a little pond, and then begins the return leg on Harkney Hill Road. You pass the Quidneck Reservoir, surrounded by forests and some cabins belonging to summer camps. The road winds through deep woods for two miles and then plunges down the greatest descent of the ride. As you begin to go downhill, enjoy the sweeping view of the countryside. Just beyond the bottom of the hill, cross two narrow inlets

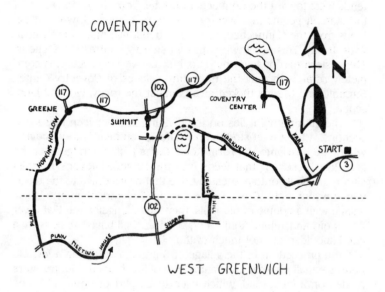

COVENTRY

GREENE

117 117 102 117 117

Hopkins Hollow

Summit

Coventry Center

Hill Farm

Hackney Hill

START
3

Plain

Plain Meeting House

Weaver Hill

Sharpe

102

N

WEST GREENWICH

How to get there: From I-95, exit north onto Route 3 and go two miles to Burger King on left.

Directions for the ride: 28 miles

- Right out of parking lot for 1.1 miles to Harkney Hill Road.
- Bear right for 0.2 mile to Hill Farm Road.
- Turn right. After 3 miles, the main road curves sharply right in Coventry Center. Continue 0.1 mile to crossroads (Route 117).
- Straight for 0.7 mile to end (Route 117 again).
- Right for 3.1 miles to crossroads (Route 102).
- Straight and then immediately left on Old Summit Road. Go 0.3 mile to end. Country store on corner. Here the short ride turns left.
- Right for 0.1 mile to crossroads (Route 117).
- Left for 2.6 miles to where Route 117 turns right.
- Go straight. After 2.2 miles, main road curves sharply left up steep hill. Continue 2.1 miles to crossroads.
- Left for 3.7 miles to crossroads (Route 102).
- Straight for 1.7 miles to Weaver Hill Road, at top of hill.
- Left for 0.6 mile to end.
- Left (still Weaver Hill Road) for 1.8 miles to end (Harkney Hill Road).
- Right for 3.6 miles to end (Route 3).
- Left for 1.1 miles to Burger King on left.

Directions for the ride: 16 miles

- Follow first 6 directions of long ride, to end of Old Summit Road.
- Left for 0.7 mile to end; left for 0.1 mile to crossroads (Route 102).
- Straight on Harkney Hill Road for 5.4 miles to end (merge left on Route 3).
- Bear left for 1.1 miles to Burger King on left.

of the Flat River Reservoir and rejoin Route 3 a mile from the starting point.

The long ride heads farther west along Route 117, now a narrow secondary road, to the picturesque village of Greene, only two miles from the Connecticut line. Here you turn south on a rustic lane that twists past rambling old farmhouses and untouched Tillinghast Pond. You must tackle a short but very steep hill which greets you just as you go around a sharp curve. Continue into West Greenwich with its small, simple church dating from 1750. Turn east on Plain Meeting House Road for the most challenging section of the ride. You drop quickly into a hollow, but then fight your way out up one of the longest hills in Rhode Island, ascending 350 feet in nearly a mile. At the summit you can breathe a sigh of relief, because the rest of the ride along narrow back roads is easy, except for one more steep hill about a quarter-mile long. You rejoin the short ride just before the glorious downhill run back to Route 3.

17. Hope Valley—Hopkinton—
North Stonington, Connecticut

Number of miles: 23 (38 with Connecticut extension)
Terrain: The short ride is rolling with two hills. The long ride is
   hilly, with some long, gradual climbs and two difficult ones.
Start: A & P, Route 138, Hope Valley, just west of I-95.
Food: Restaurant at junction of Route 216 and I-95, at state line.
   Several restaurants on Route 138 near end.

The area straddling the Rhode Island-Connecticut border is challenging for biking but inspiringly beautiful. It is a region of pristine
villages, high ridges with superb views from their summits, and
broad expanses of farmland full of cows and horses. This ride in the
southwestern portion of the state and extending into North
Stonington, Connecticut, abounds with smooth, traffic-free back
roads where the effort of some long climbs will be counterbalanced
by several glorious downhill runs.

   The ride begins in Hope Valley (also called Wyoming), a small
town on the Wood River about five miles from the Connecticut
border. At the beginning of the ride, you pass a fine, curving dam
across the river, and a well-known landmark, the Hack and Livery
General Store. This is actually a crafts and gift shop, with a cozy
atmosphere and a penny-candy counter. As you leave town you
pass another dam and a brick mill, built in 1869.

   The next town on the ride is Woodville, one of the most picturesque villages in the state. Here the Wood River flows over a small
dam flanked by three old, gracious, frame houses. After a sharp
climb out of the valley, you pass a sawmill and pull into Hopkinton,
another small, attractive village. Clustered near the main crossroads are a small white church, the town hall, the impressive Heri-
tage Playhouse, and several lovely homes, including one dated
1780. A mile west of the village you enter Connecticut and enjoy a
long descent to a prosperous dairy farm, with sweeping views of
the neighboring hillsides.

   Just ahead, the short ride angles back to the Rhode Island line
through broad farms with lots of grazing dairy cows. At the border,

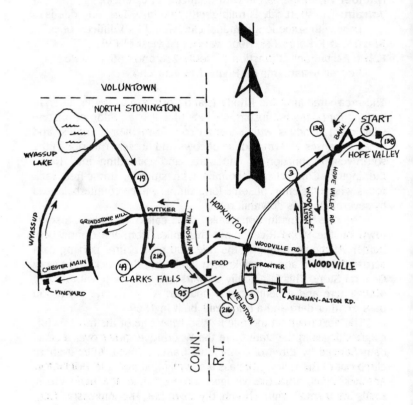

How to get there: From Route I-95, exit west onto Route 138. A & P is just ahead on right. From the east on Route 138, go to I-95 interchange. A & P is just past interchange on right.

Directions for the ride: 38 miles

- Right out of parking lot for 0.2 mile to traffic light (Route 3).
- Job left and immediately right on Arcadia Road for 0.2 mile to end, at small traffic island (Bank Street on left).
- Left for a half mile to end (merge right onto Routes 3 and 138).
- Bear right for 0.4 mile to a road that bears left where Route 138 turns right and Route 3 goes straigt uphill.
- Bear left for 3.5 miles to Woodville Road on right (large field on far corner).
- Right for 4.3 miles to crossroads and stop sign (Route 3).
- Straight for 2.3 miles to crossroads (Dension Hill Road). Here the short ride turns left.
- Right for 1.1 miles to Puttker Road. Go left for one mile to crossroads (Route 49).
- Straight on Grindstone Hill Road for 0.3 mile to fork.
- Bear left for 1.6 miles to Chester Maine Road on right.
- Right for 2 miles to end (Wyassup Road). (**Caution:** End comes up suddenly at bottom of hill.)
- Turn right and immediately curve right up hill for 4.8 miles to end (Route 49).
- Right for 3.7 miles to fork where Route 49 turns right and Route 216 bears left.
- Bear left for 1.2 miles to crossroads (Denison Hill Road).
- Right for 1.2 miles to crossroads (truck stop on corner).
- Straight for 0.6 mile to Wellstown Road.
- Sharp left for 0.6 miles to end (Route 3).
- Left for 0.2 mile to Frontier Road. Right for 0.4 mile to end. Right for 0.3 mile to Ashaway-Alton Road.
- Left for 1.5 miles to crossroads (Tomaquag Road). Straight for 1.3 miles to Woodville-Alton Road, just before end.
- Left for 1.5 miles to crossroads (Woodville Road). Straight for 2.3 miles to end (Route 3).
- Right for 2.5 miles to traffic light where Route 138 bears right and Route 3 goes straight. Bear right for 0.2 mile to A & P on left.

Directions for the ride: 23 miles

- Follow first 7 directions of long ride to crossroads (Denison Hill Road).
- Left for 1.2 miles to crossroads (truck stop on corner).
- Follow last 6 directions of long ride, beginning "Staight for 0.6 mile to Wellstown Road."

the truck stop at the I-95 interchange is a good place to rest. You now return to Hope Valley along rural roads, eventually coming to Route 3 approximately two miles south of town. You'll pedal along an open ridge with a spectacular view to your right. Finish with a long, smooth descent back into Hope Valley, passing the Enchanted Forest, a children's amusement park with a fairyland theme.

The long ride heads farther west into the magnificent ridge-and-valley country of eastern Connecticut. Rolling, open hillsides alternate with wooded glens as you wind your way westward. Chester Maine Road climbs gradually onto a high, open ridge with a full circle of sweeping views, and descends smoothly down the far side. At the top of the hill is the Crosswoods Vineyards, which is open for tours between noon and 4:30 on weekends by appointment (phone: 203-535-2205). Wyassup Road presents the most challenging section of the ride. You struggle up three long hills, two of them quite steep, but swooping descents lie between them. At the bottom of the first hill, unspoiled Wyassup Lake lies beside the road on your left. At the top of the third hill is Route 49, with the graceful Pendleton Hill Church just to the left of the intersection.

Route 49 heads south along several miles of gentle downhill grade, a welcome respite from the rigors of Wyassup Road. The route turns east to the lovely hamlet of Clarks Falls, following a slender millpond with a small dam at each end. An old gristmill stands beside the second dam. Just beyond Clarks Falls you rejoin the short ride, a mile before the truck stop at the state line.

18. That Dam Ride:
Hope Valley—Exeter—Rockville—Woodville

Number of miles: 17 (27 with Rockville—Woodville extension)
Terrain: Rolling with two tough hills.
Start: A & P supermarket, Route 138, Hope Valley, just west of
I-95.
Food: No food stops on the route. Several snack bars on Route
138 at end.

This is an original ride of the Narragansett Bay Wheelmen and one
of my personal favorites. It explores a very rural, wooded part of
South County along the Connecticut border, going past tumbling
brooks, millponds, and several fine dams. A long section of the ride
runs through the wooded Arcadia Management Area, the largest
expanse of state-owned land in Rhode Island.

Begin the ride in Hope Valley and head north for a short distance on Route 3. On your left is Wyoming Pond, a millpond formed
by a dam on the Wood River that you'll see at the end of the ride.
Just ahead, cross the river and turn north on Old Nooseneck Hill
Road, a good secondary road with almost no traffic. Follow the
swift-moving river and cross it again; there's a lovely dam on your
left. A mile farther, the main road turns right, but if you'd like to
venture off the route, go straight for a quarter mile to the Tomaquag Indian Museum. In addition to showing exhibits, the museum
also serves as a cultural center for the Narragansett Indian community, with a trading post and classes in Indian crafts and history.
Next to the museum is the Dovecrest, a restaurant run by Indians.

Back on the main road, you enter the Arcadia Management
Area, an extensive woodland area crisscrossed by hiking trails.
You'll enjoy Browning Mill Pond, with its small beach and lovely
brook that cascades under the road into the pond. Turn west onto
Route 165, which runs through the Management Area for several
miles. As you are pedaling along, you go around a curve and suddenly a steep, half-mile-long hill slants skyward in front of you. For
encouragement, however, there's a downhill run of equal magnitude

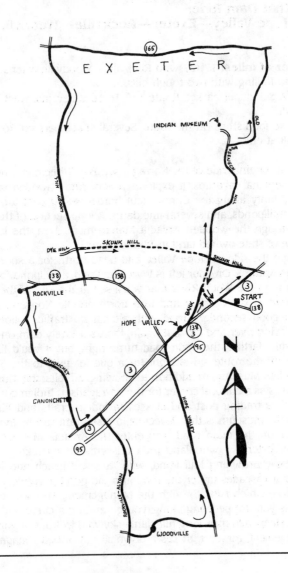

How to get there: Same as Ride 17.

Directions for the ride: 27 miles

- Right out of parking lot for 0.2 mile to traffic light (Route 3).
- Sharp right for 0.8 mile to diagonal crossroads at church (Skunk Hill Road).
- Sharp left for 0.7 mile to crossroads (Old Nooseneck Hill Road).
- Right for 2.3 miles to where main road curves 90 degrees right uphill and a smaller road goes straight.
- Right for 2.4 miles to end (Route 165).
- Left for 3.9 miles to crossroads (Escoheag Hill Road on right, Woody Hill Road on left).
- Left for 3.5 miles to crossroads (Dye Hill Road on right). Here the short ride turns left.
- Straight for 0.6 mile to crossroads (Route 138).
- Right for 0.9 mile to fork where Route 138 bears right and a secondary road bears left into Rockville.
- Bear left for 0.1 mile to Canonchet Road, left again for 0.4 mile to fork.
- Bear left (still Canonchet Road) for 1.8 miles to stop sign (Stubtown Road on right). Straight for 1.1 miles to wide crossroads (Route 3).
- Left for a half mile to divided road on right (sign says to I-95).
- Right for 2.3 miles to crossroads (Woodville Road).
- Left for 1.4 miles to end (Hope Valley Road).
- Left for 3.3 miles to fork at top of hill.
- Bear right on main road for 0.2 mile to end.
- Bear right onto Route 3 for 0.4 mile to Bank Street (unmarked) which bears left.
- Bear left for a half mile to Arcadia Road (unmarked) on right, at small traffic island.
- Right for 0.2 mile to end (Routes 3 and 138).
- Turn left and immediately bear right at traffic light. Go 0.2 mile to parking lot on left.

Directions for the ride: 17 miles

- Follow first 7 directions of long ride, to crossroads (Dye Hill Road on right).
- Left for 2.7 miles to crossroads (Old Nooseneck Hill Road).
- Right for a half mile to fork, at small traffic island.
- Bear left on Arcadia Road for 0.2 mile to end (Routes 3 and 138).
- Follow last direction of long ride.

on the other side. The route turns south onto Woody Hill Road, a narrow lane twisting through evergreen forests and a few small farms. There's a steep but much shorter hill, with a nice view at the summit, followed by a lazy descent.

Finish the short ride by heading east on Skunk Hill Road past pleasant patches of open farmland and the Kay Dee Company, which prints designs on fine linen goods. Just before the end of the ride is the impressive, gently curving dam at the base of Wyoming Pond.

The long ride proceeds farther south to Route 138, where you pedal by two small ponds and the handsome red-brick Centerville mill. Just ahead, turn onto a back road through Rockville, a tiny village with a short row of frame houses with peaked roofs, and an old stone mill. The ride continues south on Canonchet Road, a wooded lane that leads mostly downhill to Route 3. You pass undeveloped Ashville Pond and go through Canonchet, another minuscule village with a few old homes and a small stone mill that is now a plastics factory. Soon you coast downhill into Woodville, the most attractive of the mill villages on the ride, with three gracious wooden homes overlooking a fine dam on the Wood River. As you descend into the village, slow down to appreciate this picturesque spot.

The last stretch to Hope Valley goes along a smooth, mostly flat road. Just before town there's a brick mill built in 1869 with yet another dam beside it. You pass the Hack and Livery General Store, a crafts and gift shop with a big selection of penny candy. Just before the end, you see one last dam at the base of Wyoming Pond.

19. Richmond—Exeter—Carolina—Shannock

Number of miles: 21 (30 with Carolina-Shannock extension)
Terrain: Rolling, with one long hill.
Start: A & P, Route 138, Hope Valley, just west of I-95.
Food: Country store and snack bar in Shannock, on long ride.
  Store at Wawaloam Campground, Gardner Road, Richmond.
  Several restaurants on Route 138 near starting point.

This is a scenic, relaxing ride through rural Rhode Island at its finest. The south-central portion of the state contains a harmonious mixture of woods and open land rising and falling across small ridges and valleys. A network of smooth, nearly traffic-free country roads traverses the region, providing ideal conditions for cycling. You'll pedal through the Arcadia Management Area, a large tract of woodland with a small beach. The long ride includes the old mill villages of Carolina, with its distinctive octagon house, and Shannock, with stately old homes and an old fashioned country store with a soda fountain.

Start once again from Hope Valley, head east briefly on Route 138, and turn onto a back road which climbs gradually onto a ridge with a good view. Continue on to Route 112, where you'll see the Richmond Town House (the town hall), and the Bell School House, built in 1826. A mile ahead are the Washington County Fairgrounds, which host a country fair every August.

Continuing south on Route 112, stop to observe the octagonal house on your left just past a crossroads. Just ahead cross the Pawcatuck River, where the fragile shell of what was once an old wooden mill stands on the right. On the far side of the river is the village of Carolina, with a cluster of well-maintained frame houses and a small white church.

Just ahead turn east and bike through Shannock, a fine mill village with a grouping of gracious houses along the Pawcatuck River. Here the ride turns left, but if you go straight for a hundred yards you'll see a unique horseshoe-shaped dam. The stone shell of the mill, destroyed by fire, stands on your right just before the dam.

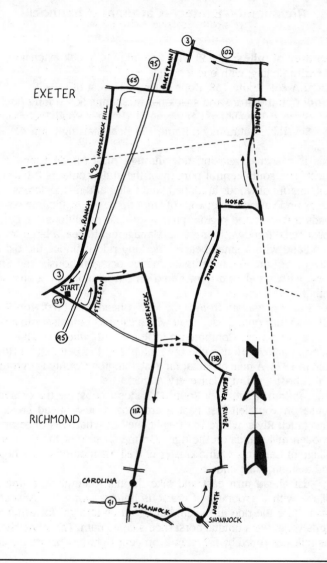

EXETER

RICHMOND

How to get there: Same as Ride 17.

Directions for the ride: 30 miles

- Turn left out of parking lot and go a half mile to Stilson Road, shortly after I-95.
- Turn left. After 0.7 mile road turns 90 degrees right. Go one mile to end (Nooseneck Road).
- Right for 1.7 miles to crossroads (Route 138). Here the short ride turns left.
- Straight on Route 112 for 3.7 miles to Shannock Road on left, immediately after you go over a railroad bridge.
- Left for 0.6 mile to fork (Sand Plain Road bears right).
- Bear left for 0.9 mile to second left, shortly after Shannock Spa. (Horseshoe-shaped dam is 100 yards straight ahead.)
- Left for 1.2 miles to end (merge right downhill).
- Bear right for 0.1 mile to Beaver River Road.
- Left for 2.1 miles to end (Route 138).
- Left for 1.1 miles to Hillsdale Road.
- Right for 3.2 miles to Hoxie Road, about a mile after James Trail.
- Right for one mile to end (merge right at top of hill onto Gardner Road).
- Sharp left for 2.5 miles to end (Ten Rod Road).
- Right for 0.1 mile to first left; go left for 0.6 mile to end (Route 102). (**Caution:** Downhill stop at end.)
- Left for 1.6 miles to Route 3.
- Left for 0.2 mile to first right; right for 0.2 mile to first left (Black Plain Road); left for 0.9 mile to end (Route 165).
- Right for 1.4 miles to Old Nooseneck Hill Road on left, at bottom of hill.
- Left for 1.8 miles to where main road curves 90 degrees right and small road (K.G. Ranch Road) goes straight.
- Straight for 2 miles to diagonal crossroads (Route 3).
- Bear right for one mile to traffic light (Route 138 on left).
- Sharp left for 0.2 mile to parking lot on left.

Directions for the ride: 21 miles

- Follow first 3 directions of long ride, to Route 138.
- Left for 0.8 mile to Hillsdale Road on left.
- Left for 3.2 miles to Hoxie Road, about a mile after James Trail.
- Follow last 10 directions of long ride, beginning "Right for one mile to end . . ."

113

The Shannock Spa, an old-time country store with a soda fountain, is a good spot for a stop.

Turn north out of Shannock, pedaling on idyllic lanes through the valley of the Beaver River, actually just a small stream. Attractive farms, with stone walls and grazing horses, slope from the road down to the river. Head west briefly on Route 138 to rejoin the short ride, and then continue north on curving, wooded back roads, passing two small ponds and a cascading brook. After a long, gradual climb, descend sharply to Route 102 and then tackle the toughest hill of the ride as you turn west to Route 3.

The rest of the ride is mostly downhill. A smooth, steady descent on Route 165 brings you into Arcadia Management Area, the largest state reservation in Rhode Island. It consists of forested hills laced with hiking trails and several small ponds. Turn south and pass Browning Mill Pond, which has a small beach. From here, it's three miles back to Hope Valley on a narrow lane through evergreen forests, and a run along Wyoming Pond.

20. East Greenwich—North Kingstown— Goddard Park

Number of miles: 16 (24 with North Kingstown extension)
Terrain: Rolling, with several short hills.
Start: East Greenwich Shopping Center, Route 1, East Greenwich, just south of Route 401.
Food: Burger King, Route 1 at Newcomb Road, North Kingstown. Snack bar at corner of Forge Road and Route 1, East Greenwich.

Just south of Warwick, as the Providence metropolitan area begins to thin out, pleasant bicycling abounds on smooth, lightly-traveled roads winding through the rocky wooded landscape. The short ride explores East Greenwich, which boasts the highest per-capita income of the Rhode Island towns. The center of town, along Route 1, retains the ambience of a turn-of-the-century community with its brick commercial buildings. Of historic interest are the Kent County Courthouse, built in 1750 and enlarged in 1805; and the fortress-like Varnum Memorial Armory, containing a military museum. Old homes, many built over a century ago, perch on the steep hillside between Route 1 and the bay. West of town, most of the newer homes lie on large wooded lots, well-integrated with the landscape, giving a rustic rather than a suburban flavor to the area.

Begin the ride by heading along the waterfront on Greenwich Cove, a small inlet of Greenwich Bay, which is in turn an inlet of Narragansett Bay. The slender, sheltered cove is an ideal spot to moor small boats. You bike past several marinas and some old waterfront buildings recycled into cozy restaurants and taverns. Then head inland, climbing a short, steep hill just after you cross Route 1.

As you head west on Middle Road, the landscape becomes more and more suburban; and after you cross Route 2 it becomes rural. Tillinghast Road is a delight as you roll up and over small hills. The short ride turns east on busier Frenchtown Road. You pass Browne and Sharpe Manufacturing Company, makers of machine tools and hydraulic equipment. During the early 1980s, the

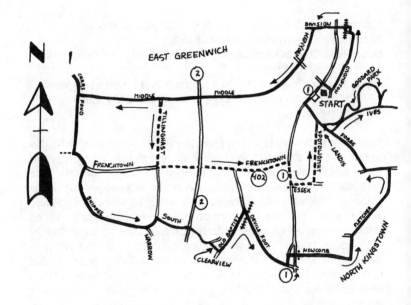

How to get there: From the north, head south on I-95 to Route 4, bear left, and just ahead take the Route 401 exit. Turn right (east) at end of ramp and go 2½ miles to traffic light (Route 1). Turn right, and shopping center is just ahead on left. From the south, exit south from I-95 onto Route 2, and immediately turn left on Route 401. Go 2½ miles to traffic light (Route 1). Turn right, and shopping center is just ahead on left. By bike from Providence, head south on Elmwood Avenue to where Reservoir Avenue bears right. Straight for 3.4 miles to end (merge right on Route 1, Post Road). Bear right; go about 7 miles to parking lot on left, just beyond Route 401.

Directions for the ride: 24 miles

- Right on Route 1 for 0.1 mile to traffic light (Rocky Hollow Road on right).
- Right for 0.1 mile to railroad tracks (**Caution** here). Shift into low gear before you get to tracks. Note: This railroad crossing may be blocked off in the future. If so, continue north on Route 1 for a half mile to King Street, and turn right to waterfront, which is worth seeing. Ride resumes by turning west (uphill) from Route 1 on Division Street.
- Bear left immediately after tracks. After 0.7 mile, road turns 90 degrees left on King Street.
- Jog left and immediately right along water. Just ahead road turns 90 degrees left and crosses tracks (**Caution** again). Go 0.2 mile to traffic light (Route 1). If tracks are blocked off, backtrack to King Street, which goes underneath them. Follow King Street to Route 1, right to traffic light (Division Street), and left uphill.
- Straight for 0.4 mile to Kenyon Avenue, shortly after top of hill.
- Left for 0.3 mile to crossroads and stop sign (Route 401).
- Straight for 2.3 miles to traffic light (Route 2). (**Caution** crossing Route 401.)
- Straight for one mile to Tillinghast Road on left. Here the short ride turns left.
- Curve right for 1.7 miles to end (Carr's Pond Road).
- Left for 1.3 miles to end, where main road turns left and Bates Trail turns right. Left for a half mile to stop sign.
- Right on Shippee Road for 1.8 miles to where Narrow Lane turns right and main road curves left.
- Curve left for 0.6 mile to stop sign (Tillinghast Road bears left, South Road turns right).
- Right for 0.9 mile to traffic light (Route 2). Straight for a half mile to fork at top of hill; bear right on Clearview Drive for 0.3 mile to end (Old Baptist Road).
- Left for 1.3 miles to railroad overpass on right (Devils Foot Road).
- Sharp right across overpass for 1.3 miles to Namcook Road on left (motel on far corner).
- Sharp left for 0.1 mile to Newcomb Road on right. (Burger King on right just before Newcomb Road. Enter and leave by back entrance. **Caution:** Speed bumps.)

117

- Turn right and immediately cross Route 1 at traffic light. After 1.1 miles road turns 90 degrees left. Continue 0.6 mile to stop sign.
- Bear right on Fletcher Road for 1.7 miles to end (North Quidnisset Road).
- Left for 0.4 mile to Forge Road. Right for 1.1 miles to unmarked road on right, just before restaurant (first right after bridge).
- Right for 1.5 miles to Goddard Park entrance.
- Left for 0.4 mile to fork. Here ride bears left, but if you bear right for 0.3 mile you come to the beach.
- Bear left for 1.5 miles to end (park exit).
- Right for one mile to Route 1.
- Bear right, then immediately turn right on Greenwich Boulevard for a quarter mile to end (Route 1 again).
- Right for 0.1 mile to starting point on right.

Directions for the ride: 16 miles

- Follow first 9 directions of long ride, to Tillinghast Road on left.
- Left for 1.3 miles to crossroads (Frenchtown Road).
- Left for one mile to traffic light (Route 2).
- Straight for 1.4 miles to end (Route 1).
- Right for a half mile to Essex Road on left (traffic light).
- Left for 0.4 mile to Potowomut Road.
- Left for one mile to Landis Drive on right. Notice dam on left after 0.2 mile. Right for a quarter mile to end.
- Right for 100 yards, then left for 1.5 miles to Goddard Park entrance on left.
- Follow last 5 directions of long ride.

firm was on strike for nearly two years—one of the longest strikes in American labor history.

Proceed into the Potowomut section of Warwick, a peninsula whose northern shore fronts on both Greenwich Cove and Greenwich Bay, and is included within Goddard Memorial State Park. A recreational showpiece and a pleasure for biking, the park was originally two country estates and contains nearly 500 acres of lawns, stately forest, and beach. On the grounds are a golf course, riding academy, and miles of bridle paths. When you leave the park, you're only a couple of miles from the start.

The long ride first follows the ups and downs of Middle Road westward until its end; then a well-earned downhill run on Carr's Pond Road will reward your efforts. More downhills await you most of the way to Route 2. The stretch between Routes 2 and 1 is more suburban. After crossing Route 1, parallel North Kingstown's Quonset Point base, where that hallmark of military architecture, the Quonset Hut, originated. At present, most of Quonset Point is deactivated and open to the public. On the base, miles of roads pass by gigantic runways, docks, grim military buildings, and Electric Boat's plant.

North of Quonset Point, you pedal through an area of gracious country estates and gentleman farms. After a relaxing descent to the Hunt River, rejoin the short ride for the circuit of Goddard Park and the return to the starting point.

21. Wickford—Kingston

Number of miles: 14 (29 with Kingston extension)
Terrain: Gently rolling.
Start: Town Dock, end of Main Street, Wickford.
Food: Groceries in Kingston and West Kingston on Route 138.
    Country store at corner of Route 2 and Allenton Road.

On this ride you'll explore a section of southern Rhode Island just inland from the west shore of Narragansett Bay. Both Wickford and Kingston are historic communities with handsome homes dating back to the early 1800s. In Kingston you will bike through the large, impressive campus of the University of Rhode Island, with its blend of traditional stone buildings and stark modern ones.

The picturesque harbor town of Wickford is a delightful place to start the ride. The town boasts an impressive collection of early nineteenth-century homes and hosts the state's largest art festival in July. As you leave the dock on Main Street, take a good look at all the houses, many with plaques indicating when they were built. Also on Main Street you pass the stately Old Narragansett Church, which dates from 1707, the oldest Episcopal church north of Virginia.

Turn off Main Street and go through the center of town. On your right is the Wickford Diner, an authentic dining-car eatery sandwiched between two newer buildings. It's a good spot for a bite after the ride. Just ahead cross the small bridge over the head of the boat-filled harbor. It's worth dismounting for a minute to savor the view of the town from the left side of the bridge. Just beyond the bridge is the red-brick North Kingstown Town Hall, built in 1888, on your left. (Wickford is part of North Kingstown.)

Two miles out of town make a small loop along the bay shore, and take in the view of the Jamestown Bridge. The short ride now heads inland past small farms and estates hidden behind stone walls. The northbound leg on Lafayette Road is a delight as it winds through prosperous farmland over small rolling hills. The deserted-looking building marked "King of Clubs" comes alive with country-and-Western music at night. Just after crossing Route 4, you will

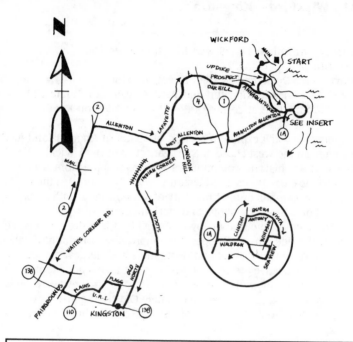

How to get there: From the north, head south on I-95 to Route 4 (exit on left). Go about 2 miles to Route 403 exit; then go south for about 2.5 miles to Route 1. Turn left (south), go about 2 miles to Route 1A, and bear left (sign says Wickford). After a half mile bear slightly left where Route 1A turns right. Go 0.4 mile to dock, at end. From the southwest on I-95, exit east onto Route 102 for about 11 miles to Route 1, at traffic light (go straight at both rotaries). Cross Route 1 and go a half mile to fork (Route 1A bears right). Bear left for 0.2 mile, through downtown Wickford, to end. Turn right to dock. From the south, head north on Route 1 to Route 102 (traffic light). Right for a half mile to fork (Route 1A bears right). Bear left for 0.2 mile, through downtown Wickford, to end. Turn right to dock.

Directions for the ride: 29 miles

- Head away from dock on Main Street for 0.3 mile to stop sign. Left on Brown Street for 0.2 mile to fork. Bear left on Route 1A for 0.2 mile to first right, Updike Street.
- Bear right for 0.1 mile to end (Prospect Avenue).
- Right for 0.6 mile to end (Annaquatucket Road).
- Left for one mile to end (Route 1A).
- Left for 0.1 mile to Waldron Avenue; go right for 0.3 mile to Clinton Drive, which bears left. Take it for 0.2 mile to Anthony Drive.
- Right for 0.2 mile to fork (Winsor Avenue bears right).
- Bear left along water for 0.3 mile to end (Winsor Avenue).
- Left for 0.1 mile to crossroads (Waldron Avenue).
- Left for 100 yards to end (Sea View Avenue), at bay.
- Turn right, following bay on left. Just ahead road turns 90 degrees right. Go 0.2 mile to end (merge left at stop sign on Waldron Avenue).
- Bear left for 0.4 mile to end (Route 1A).
- Left for 0.3 mile to second right (Hamilton-Allenton Road).
- Right for 1.5 miles to end (Route 1).
- Right for 0.2 mile to West Allenton Road; go left for a half mile to traffic light at Route 4. Continue straight for one mile to fork where main road bears right uphill.
- Bear right for a half mile to another fork (Indian Corner Road turns left, Exeter Road bears right). Here the short ride bears right.
- Turn left for 3.4 miles to end.
- Right for 0.4 mile to Old North Road; left for 1.5 miles to end (Route 138).
- Right for 0.2 mile to traffic light. Right on Upper College Road for 0.7 mile to end (Flagg Road).
- Left for 0.6 mile to end. Left for 0.2 mile to end (Plains Road).
- Right for 0.9 mile to traffic light (Route 138).
- Right for 0.6 mile to crossroads immediately after railroad overpass (Fairgrounds Road).
- Right for 0.4 mile to crossroads (Waites Corner Road).
- Left for 0.8 mile to fork. Bear right for 100 yards to Route 2.
- Right for 4.1 miles to second crossroads (Exeter Mall on corner).

- Right for 1.8 miles to Lafayette Road, shortly after Dry Bridge Road.
- Left for 1.7 miles to fork while going uphill. (Oak Hill Road bears right).
- Bear right for 0.1 mile to traffic light (Route 4); straight for 1.4 miles to end (Route 1).
- Left for 0.3 mile to Annaquatucket Road. Right for half mile to Prospect Avenue.
- Left for 0.7 mile to Updike Street. Bear left for 0.1 mile to Route 1A.
- Left for 0.2 mile to fork (downtown Wickford on right).
- Bear right for 0.2 mile to end (Main Street).
- Right for 0.1 mile to first right (Gold Street).
- Right for 0.2 mile back to Main Street. Right to dock.

Directions for the ride: 14 miles
- Follow first 15 directions of long ride, to fork where Indian Corner Road turns left and Exeter Road bears right.
- Bear right for 0.2 mile to Lafayette Road.
- Bear right for 1.7 miles to fork, while going uphill (Oak Hill Road bears right).
- Follow last 7 directions of long ride.

ride alongside Secret Lake, a good spot for a rest about three miles from the end.

The long ride turns south along Indian Corner Road, midway between Wickford and Kingston, and passes through extensive turf farms stretching to the horizon in a velvety green blanket. Slocum Road ascends gradually onto Kingston Hill, the long ridge where the village of Kingston and the University of Rhode Island are located. You enter Kingston on North Road, a byway so quiet that it is hard to believe that a major university with over ten thousand students is a quarter-mile away.

Kingston is refreshingly unique for a college town in that it is almost completely undeveloped. Even the main drag, Route 138, is uncommercialized and safe for riding. The commercial areas and most of the local population are centered in Wakefield, three miles south.

At the end of North Road in the center of town, turn right on Route 138. Notice the fine homes on both sides of the road, most dating back to 1800. Just ahead turn into the University of Rhode Island campus, passing elegant fraternity houses and the handsome stone buildings adjoining the main quadrangle on your left. The remainder of the campus slopes down the west side of Kingston Hill, and at the bottom of the hill are broad farms run by the College of Agriculture. A mile ahead you pedal through West Kingston, passing the railroad station and the granite Washington County Courthouse with its stately clock tower.

Continue on through more farmland to Route 2, a flat road with a good shoulder. You will follow Route 2 for several miles, and then turn east onto Allenton Road. At the intersection is the Exeter Mall—not a gleaming shopping center, but a cluttered country store. Allenton Road is a pleasant run through wide stretches of gently rolling farmland. At the next intersection turn north on Lafayette Road, rejoining the short ride.

22. Bay and Beaches: Wakefield—Narragansett Pier—Bonnet Shores—Saunderstown

Number of miles: 17 (26 with Saunderstown extension)
Terrain: Gently rolling, with one vicious hill.
Start: Salt Pond Shopping Center, corner of Route 108 and Woodruff Avenue, Narragansett.
Food: Several stores and snack bars on Route 1A. Pizza at end.

On this ride you'll explore the southern reaches of Narragansett Bay where it empties into the Atlantic Ocean. The first half of the ride follows the coastline, looping around the scenic headland of Bonnet Shores and through the historic community of Saunderstown to the birthplace of Gilbert Stuart. The return trip heads inland past gentleman farms bordered by stone walls and rustic wooden fences.

The ride starts from the edge of Wakefield, the only large town in southern Rhode Island between Westerly and Narragansett Bay. Much of its economy is related to the University of Rhode Island, four miles to the north. From Wakefield, you head a short distance eastward to the gracious seaside town of Narragansett Pier. Just before you reach the ocean you pass the base of a water tower, originally two hundred feet high, which was destroyed during the 1938 hurricane.

During the Gilded Age around the turn of the century, Narragansett Pier was a miniature Newport with huge Victorian resort hotels lining its seashore. Unfortunately, none remain. The town's major landmark from that era is the Towers, a stone building forming an arch across the road. This is the last remaining segment of the Narragansett Casino, designed in 1882 by Stanford White. Today the structure houses the Narragansett Chamber of Commerce.

After pedaling underneath the Towers, head northward along the bay, going inland a few hundred feet and up onto a ridge overlooking the bay. After a few miles, you turn onto a side road that loops around Bonnet Shores, a rocky promontory jutting into Narragansett Bay with fine homes overlooking the water. The short ride then turns inland and descends to the Pettaquamscutt River

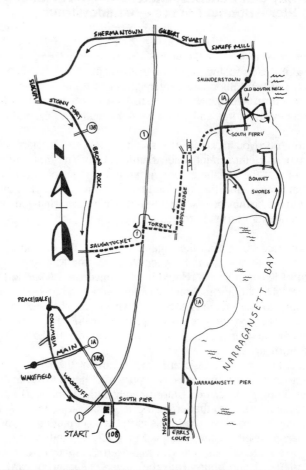

How to get there: From the north, take Route 1 to the Route 108, Point Judith, Scarborough exit. Bear right at end of ramp; shopping center is just ahead on right. From the south, take Route 1 to Route 108 exit. Turn right at end of exit ramp and shopping center is just ahead on right.

Directions for the ride: 25 miles

- Left out of parking lot onto Route 108 for 0.1 mile to traffic light.
- Right on South Pier Road for 1.2 miles to crossroads and stop sign.
- Right on Gibson Avenue for 0.2 mile to Earls Court; left for 0.3 mile to end (Ocean Road).
- Left for 0.9 mile to end, at traffic light. You'll go underneath the Towers.
- Bear right along water for 3.8 miles to traffic light (sign says Bonnet Shores).
- Turn right. Just ahead is a fork; bear right for 2.1 miles to another fork where the main road bears left and a smaller road bears right along the water.
- Bear right. After 0.2 mile, road turns 90 degrees left. Go 0.2 mile to first left.
- Left for 0.2 mile to third crossroads.
- Right for 0.7 mile to traffic light (Route 1A).
- Right for 0.8 mile to traffic light (South Ferry Road on right). Here the short ride turns left.
- Right for 0.4 mile to crossroads (Ray Trainor Drive on right, Old Boston Neck Road on left).
- Left for a quarter mile to Crosswinds Drive.
- Right for a quarter mile to Horizon Drive (second right).
- Right for a quarter mile to end (Searidge Drive).
- Left for 0.1 mile to Crosswinds Drive. Left for 0.3 mile to crossroads (Wyndcliff Drive). Right for 0.2 mile to end (Old Boston Neck Road). Right for a half mile to crossroads (Route 1A).
- Bear right for 1.3 miles to Snuff Mill Road on left.
- Left for 1.2 miles to Gilbert Stuart Road on left (sign says Birthplace).
- Turn left. Gilbert Stuart's birthplace and snuff mill are on right just ahead at bottom of hill. Continue 1.1 miles to Route 1.
- Straight on Shermantown Road for 3.1 miles to end (Slocum Road). (**Caution** crossing Route 1.)
- Left for a quarter mile to end (Stony Fort Road).
- Left for 1.4 miles to Route 138.
- Straight onto Broad Rock Road for two miles to crossroads and stop sign (Saugatucket Road).

- Straight for 1.2 miles to end (Route 108).
- Right for 0.3 mile to end, in Peace Dale.
- Left on Columbia Street for 0.3 mile to fork (River Street bears right).
- Bear left (still Columbia Street) for 0.3 mile to traffic light (Main Street). Stedman's Bicycle Shop on far right corner.
- Straight for 1.1 mile to shopping center on right.

Directions for the ride: 17 miles

- Follow first 10 directions of long ride, to corner of Route 1A and South Ferry Road.
- Turn left. After 0.4 mile main road curves sharply left. Continue 0.4 mile to Middlebridge Road, just after bridge.
- Left for 1.6 miles to Torry Road. Right for a half mile to Route 1 (huff, puff, groan).
- Turn right. Just ahead make U-turn at traffic light, using ramp to cross highway at right angles. Go 0.2 mile to Saugatucket Road.
- Right for 1.2 miles to crossroads (Broad Rock Road).
- Left for 1.2 miles to end (Route 108).
- Follow last 4 directions of long ride.

(also called the Narrow River), a salt-water inlet about two miles west of the bay that runs parallel to it. You ride along the river for two miles; then you tackle a challenging hill as you turn inland from the riverbank. The last few miles continue inland past small farms and horse pastures.

The long ride continues farther north along the bay to the historic community of Saunderstown. From the hillside, superb views of the bay and the graceful span of the Jamestown Bridge unfold before you. You pass the Casey Farm, an unspoiled tract of land that has been cultivated since the Revolution. Administered by the Society for the Preservation of New England Antiquities, it has a fine collection of period furniture and memorabilia and is open from June through October. Just past the farm turn inland to view another historic landmark, the Gilbert Stuart Birthplace. The country's famous portrait painter, best known for his portrait of George Washington on the dollar bill, was born here in 1755. Next to the home where he was born is the first snuff mill in the United States, built in 1751 by the artist's father.

A tough hill leads from the birthplace to Route 1. Cross this highway and return to Wakefield on back roads passing attractive farms. Shortly before the end, you pass the extensive grounds of the Saint Dominic Savio Youth Center. Just ahead is the historic village of Peace Dale, which is adjacent to Wakefield. In the center of town is a cluster of handsome stone buildings from the mid-to-late nineteenth century; be sure to notice the elegant library, built in 1891, on the right. Across the street is the Museum of Primitive Culture; hours vary depending on staff volunteers.

23. Westerly—Watch Hill—Ashaway

Number of miles: 17 (32 with Ashaway extension)
Terrain: Flat, with a couple of little hills. The long ride has one difficult climb.
Start: Benny's, junction of Route 1 and Dunns Corner Road, Westerly.
Food: Snack bar in downtown Westerly. Olympia Tea Room, Watch Hill with old fashioned, homey atmosphere—excellent place for a snack. Numerous snack bars along Misquamicut Beach in summer.
Caution: Unless you go early in the morning, it's best not to do this ride on summer weekends because of heavy beach traffic along the shore.

The southwestern corner of Rhode Island contains some of the most scenic bicycling in the state. Along the magnificent coastline are graceful old homes, resort hotels, and estates standing guard above the waves. Misquamicut Beach is one of the finest in the state. The Pawcatuck River, forming the southern boundary between Rhode Island and Connecticut, widens from a picturesque millstream to a broad estuary lined with little coves. To the north are the rolling woods and farmlands typical of the southern third of the state, fondly known as South County.

The short ride comprises the area along the Pawcatuck River estuary and the ocean. At the beginning of the ride you pass north of Winnapaug Pond, one of the larger salt ponds in the state. Just after you come to the river, you pass through the well-manicured waterfront community of Avondale and then down to Watch Hill.

Watch Hill is an old, well-to-do resort town with smart shops, elegant waterfront homes, and rambling Victorian resort hotels. The nation's earliest operating carousel, built before 1871, is located here. A footpath leads out to Napatree Point, the westernmost top of land in the state. The point, which contained a row of cottages destroyed during the 1938 hurricane, has reverted to its natural state. At its extreme southern tip is the Watch Hill Coast Guard

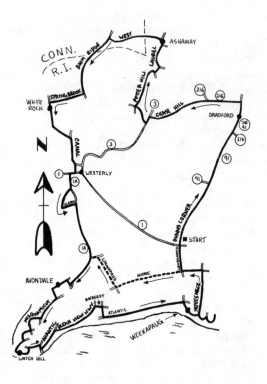

How to get there: From the north, head south on Route I-95 to Exit 1 (Route 3). Bear right at end of ramp for about 5 miles to Route 78 (Westerly Bypass). Go southeast on bypass to Route 1. Left for 2.3 miles to Benny's on left, just after traffic light. From the west, exit south from Route I-95 on Route 2. Go 1.3 miles to Route 78 (Westerly Bypass). Left (east) on bypass to Route 1. Left for 2.3 miles to Benny's on left, just past traffic light.

Directions for the ride: 17 miles

- Left out of parking lot on Dunns Corner Road. Cross Route 1 and go 0.6 mile to crossroads (Shore Road). Note: Long ride turns right out of parking lot instead of left.
- Right for 2.5 miles to crossroads (Winnapaug Road).
- Right for 0.9 mile to end (sign indicates Watch Hill).
- Left for 0.2 mile to end (Route 1A, Watch Hill Road).
- Left for one mile to where the main road curves sharply left and a side road goes straight. Go straight for 50 yards to end.
- Right for 0.2 mile to end (Pawcatuck River in front of you).
- Left for one mile to end (Watch Hill Road).
- Right for 0.6 mile to Misquamicut Road; bear right for a half mile to fork where Sequan Road bears left. Bear right uphill for 0.1 mile to crossroads.
- Turn right. Just ahead road turns 90 degrees left. Go 0.1 mile to stop sign at bottom of hill (Bay Street).
- Bear right. Follow main road for 0.7 mile to small crossroads shortly after huge wooden Ocean House (Everett Avenue, unmarked). To visit Coast Guard station, turn right after a half mile onto narrow lane. It's on the right just before you curve 90 degrees left onto Bluff Avenue. Please *walk* along the lane. It is a private road open to pedestrians only.
- Jog right on Everett Avenue and immediately left on Niantic Avenue. Go 0.3 mile to stop sign; continue straight for 0.2 mile to fork (main road bears right).
- Bear right for 1.2 miles to Bayberry Road on right. It's the first right after a long stretch with no roads on right.
- Right for 0.2 mile to crossroads (Maplewood Avenue).
- Right for 0.3 mile to end (Atlantic Avenue).
- Left for 3.1 miles to crossroads just after small bridge.
- Right along ocean for 0.8 mile to dead-end sign.
- Backtrack along ocean for 0.2 mile to second fork (Noyesneck Road bears right, main road curves left along water).
- Bear right for one mile to crossroads (Shore Road).
- Left for a half mile to crossroads (Weekapaug Road on left, Langworthy Road on right).
- Right for 0.6 mile to Route 1. Benny's is on far right corner.

Directions for the ride: 32 miles

- Right out of parking lot on Dunns Corner Road for 2.1 miles to stop sign (Route 91 on left and straight).
- Straight for 2.6 miles to Route 216 on left (sign says Ashaway).
- Left for 0.8 mile to where Route 216 curves right and Chase Hill Road goes straight, up steep hill.
- Straight for 2.3 miles to end (Route 3).
- Jog left and immediately right on Hiscox Road. Go 0.4 mile to first right (Potter Hill Road).
- Right for one mile to road on left immediately after bridge.
- Turn left. Just ahead is a fork. Bear left along river for 0.8 mile to end. Left for 100 yards to fork.
- Bear left on West Street for 1.4 miles to end (Boom Bridge Road).
- Left for 1.7 miles to Spring Brook Avenue on right.
- Right for 0.8 mile to end; left for 0.8 mile to end.
- Bear right on Canal Street for 0.7 mile to fork just after you go underneath railroad bridge.
- Bear right for 0.2 mile to end (Route 1).
- Jog right and immediately left on Route 1A. (**Caution:** Watch traffic.) After 0.1 mile, curve slightly right (sign says Beaches). Go 0.4 mile to fork (Route 1A bears left).
- Bear right along river on Margin Street for a half mile to Clark Street.
- Left for 0.3 mile to end (Route 1A).
- Right for 2.7 miles to where the main road curves sharply left and a side road goes straight. Go straight for 50 yards to end.
- Follow last 15 directions of short ride, beginning with "Right for 0.2 mile to end."

station, among the more spectacular places in Rhode Island. It offers nearly a 360-degree panorama of the Atlantic. A couple miles to the east begins Misquamicut Beach, a narrow spit between the ocean and Winnapaug Pond. Just past Misquamicut you go through the graceful oceanfront community of Weekapaug, with handsome gabled and turreted homes perched on the rocky shoreline.

The long ride starts by heading north, away from the coast, through farms and woodland to the mill village of Bradford; here you cross the Pawcatuck River into Hopkinton. Turn west on Chase Hill Road, an idyllic lane that climbs sharply and then descends back into the valley. Parallel the river to Ashaway, passing two picturesque dams. This mill village in Hopkinton is known for its manufacture of fishing line.

From Ashaway, turn west and pedal through about two miles of Connecticut. Now the landscape changes, with broad fields, full of cows, sweeping up gentle hillsides. Cross the Pawcatuck back into Rhode Island and enter the mill village of White Rock, with its striking Victorian mill built in 1849. Pedal along the river through downtown Westerly and past the point where it widens into a tidal estuary. Continue on to join the short ride for the run to Watch Hill and along the ocean.

24. South County: Kingston—Shannock Charlestown—Matunuck

Number of miles: 24 (32 with Shannock—Charlestown extension)
Terrain: Gently rolling.
Start: University of Rhode Island athletic area parking lot, Route 138, Kingston.
Food: Country store and soda fountain in Shannock. Country store in Kingston, at corner of South Road and Route 138, near end.

The southern third of Rhode Island west of Narragansett Bay consists of Washington County, which most state residents affectionately call South County. This is an area of unique beauty. The coastline, containing some of the finest beaches in the Northeast, extends along a series of narrow spits of land with the ocean on the south and, on the north, salt ponds swarming with birds. Inland is a refreshingly varied landscape of farmland and wooded hills, interspersed with ponds, swamps, and picturesque mill villages.

The ride starts from the lower edge of the U.R.I. campus at the bottom of Kingston Hill. Head south for several miles on Route 110, one of the more pleasant numbered routes in the state for cycling. As you proceed along the flat, lightly travelled road, you cross the defunct Narragansett Pier Railroad, a single-track, narrow-gauge line which once transported thousands of beachgoers before the automobile took its place. Soon you pass unspoiled Larkin Pond, and then enjoy a relaxing run along the shore of Wordens Pond, the second largest freshwater lake in the state. Here the short ride heads toward the ocean.

After crossing Route 1, you enter the broad meadows of the coastal plain. The ocean lies about a mile south, with several side roads leading down to the beaches. The ecology of the shoreline is too fragile to support a road directly along the coast, so to get down to the beach you will have to ride a small additional distance. There are several beaches you can visit. The first is Green Hill Beach, with a community of attractive summer homes on the gen-

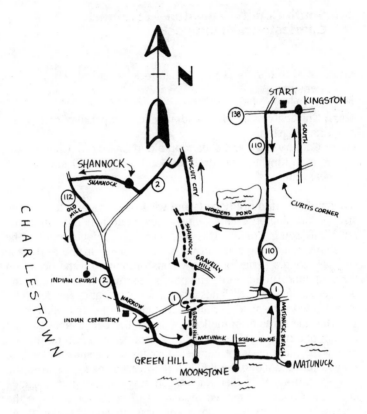

How to get there: From the north, head south on I-95 and Routes 4 and 2 to Route 138, at rotary. Turn left for two miles to parking lot on left, just past tennis courts. From the west, exit east from I-95 onto Route 138. Go about 9 miles to Route 110 on right, at traffic light. Continue on Route 138 for 0.7 mile to parking lot on left. From the east head west on Route 138 to Route 108 on left. Continue straight for 0.9 mile to parking lot on right, at bottom of hill just before tennis courts.

Directions for the ride: 32 miles

- Right out of parking lot for 0.7 mile to traffic light.
- Left on Route 110 for 3.8 miles to crossroads and blinking light.
- Right on Wordens Pond Road for 2.6 miles to Biscuit City Road on right. Here the short ride goes straight.
- Right for 1.3 miles to a new road on left. Go left for 0.4 mile to end (Route 2). Then go left for 0.6 mile to crossroads (Shannock Road).
- Right for 1.8 miles to end (Route 112).
- Left for 0.9 mile to Old Mill Road on right.
- Turn right. After 0.7 mile, road turns 90 degrees left. Continue 1.6 miles to Route 2, at end. (Dirt road on right shortly before Route 2 leads 0.7 mile to Indian Church.)
- Bear right for one mile to Narrow Lane. Left for 1.3 miles to Route 1. (After 0.7 mile, Indian cemetery on right at bottom of hill.)
- Right for 0.2 mile to U-turn slot in median strip.
- Make U-turn and go 0.2 mile to first exit (sign says Charlestown Beach). (**Caution** making U-turn.)
- Bear right. Just ahead is crossroads and stop sign. Straight for 0.3 mile to end (Matunuck Schoolhouse Road).
- Left for 1.4 miles to fork.
- Bear left (still Matunuck Schoolhouse Road) for 1.6 miles to crossroads (Moonstone Beach Road). To visit Green Hill Beach, bear right instead of left for one mile.
- Right on Moonstone Beach Road. After 0.4 mile, paved road turns 90 degrees left (dirt road goes straight ahead for 0.4 mile to Moonstone Beach). Continue 1.1 miles to end (Matunuck Beach Road).
- Left for 1.4 miles to Route 1. (To visit Matunuck Beach, turn right instead of left for 0.3 mile).
- Turn right and go to U-turn slot in median strip just ahead.
- Make U-turn and go 0.4 mile to first exit (sign says Old Post Road, Perryville). (**Caution** making U-turn.)
- Bear right for 0.3 mile to crossroads (Route 110).
- Right for 2.1 miles to crossroads and blinking light.
- Straight for 1.3 miles to Curtis Corner Road.
- Right for 1.6 miles to crossroads (South Road).

- Left for 1.8 miles to end (Route 138).
- Left for 0.8 mile to parking lot on right.

Directions for the ride: 24 miles

- Follow first 3 directions of long ride, to Biscuit City Road on right.
- Straight for 0.3 mile to end (Shannock Road).
- Left for 1.3 miles to fork where Gravelly Hill Road goes straight and Shannock Road bears right. Bear right for 1.3 miles to end (Route 1).
- Right for 0.2 mile to U-turn slot in median strip.
- Make U-turn and go 0.4 mile to first exit (sign says Green Hill Beach). (**Caution** making U-turn.)
- Right for a quarter mile to Green Hill Beach Road (first left).
- Left for 0.8 mile to end (Matunuck Schoolhouse Road).
- Turn left. Immediately ahead is a fork.
- Follow last 11 directions of long ride.

tle hillside overlooking the beach. Two miles east is Moonstone Beach, completely undeveloped and a traditional spot for skinny-dipping. Between these two beaches is Trustom Pond Wildlife Refuge, a wonderful area for bird watching. The next beach is Matunuck, the most built up and commercialized of the three. Between Moonstone and Matunuck is the popular summer theater, Theater by the Sea.

At Matunuck turn northward for the trip back to Kingston. Follow the southern half of Route 110, and then take side roads into Kingston past small farms and older homes set back from the roadway on wooded lots. When you come to Route 138 in Kingston, notice the lovely historic houses, handsome white church, and the Old Washington County Jail (now headquarters of the local Historical Society) gracing both sides of the road. Breeze down Kingston Hill to finish your ride.

The long ride heads farther west after the run along Wordens Pond. There is a gradual climb followed by a gentle descent to the headwaters of the Pawcatuck River, that flows from the pond to the southwestern corner of the state. You parallel the river briefly and come out on Route 2, where you'll see the large concrete mill building of Kenyon Industries. This is a major manufacturer of coated nylon for bike bags, panniers, and tents, and waterproofing seam-sealer. Just ahead wind through Shannock, a museum-piece mill village of rambling wooden homes with broad porches and black shutters. The Pawcatuck River flows over an unusual horseshoe-shaped dam and past the burned-out shell of the mill. The Shannock Spa, an old-fashioned country store with a soda fountain, is a good rest stop.

A few miles beyond Shannock take wooded back roads through the tribal homeland of Narragansett Indians, whose descendants are trying to regain title to several square miles of land in Charlestown. Tucked away on a dirt road off the route is the Narragansett Indian Church, a small stone structure built in 1859, which welcomes visitors at its eleven o'clock Sunday service. On Narrow Lane is the Royal Indian Burial Ground. Just ahead you cross Route 1 and parallel the southern coast through broad meadows to rejoin the short ride.

25. Wakefield—Galilee—Point Judith
Narragansett Pier—South Kingston

Number of miles: 16 (28 with South Kingston extension)
Terrain: Flat, with one monstrous hill on the long ride.
Start: Salt Pond Shopping Center, corner of Route 108 and
Woodruff Avenue, Narragansett.
Food: Aunt Carrie's, corner of Route 108 and Ocean Road. Great
seafood! Several snack bars near beaches, open during the
summer. Burger King and McDonald's on Tower Hill Road,
just east of starting point.
Caution: During the summer, traffic in the beach areas is very
heavy. Best time to ride is early in the morning or late
afternoon.

On this ride you'll explore the midpoint of Rhode Island's southern
coast, where the shoreline turns abruptly northward at Point Judith.
Views of the ocean abound as you head to the picturesque fishing
village of Galilee, and then south to the tip of the peninsula. Follow
the shore past gracious waterfront homes to Narragansett Pier,
where you'll pedal beneath the arch of The Towers, an architectural
landmark designed by Stanford White.

As in Ride 22, the ride starts just outside of Wakefield. Head
south on Route 108 down the Point Judith peninsula. A wide shoulder is finally being constructed on this busy road. As you turn west
toward Galilee, a panorama of broad salt marshes unfolds before
you. In the distance you can see Point Judith Pond, the long saltwater inlet that separates Point Judith from the mainland. Galilee, an
active fishing port that has not been overly commercialized, is the
main terminal for the ferry to Block Island. Outside of Galilee, Sand
Hill Cove Beach, one of the nicest beaches in the state, is the best
spot on the ride for a swim.

Bike to the tip of Point Judith, a broad grassy promontory com-
manded by a lighthouse and Coast Guard station, whose grounds
are open to the public. The northward run along the coast road to
Narragansett Pier is bicycle heaven. You pass crowded Scarborough
Beach, where most of Rhode Island's teenagers will be found on

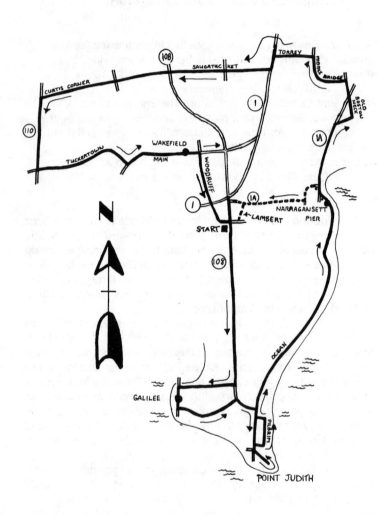

How to get there: Same as Ride 22.

Directions for the ride: 28 miles

- Right out of parking lot on Route 108 for 3.6 miles to divided road on right at traffic light (sign says Galilee, Block Island Boat). You'll go straight at several traffic lights on this stretch.
- Right for 1.1 miles to crossroads and stop sign. (Here ride goes left, but you can turn right to go around Great Island, with fine views of Point Judith Pond. This adds 3 miles to ride.)
- Left at end. After 0.4 mile road turns 90 degrees left. Continue 1.3 miles to end (Route 108).
- Right for 0.3 miles to crossroads (Ocean Road).
- Turn right. After a half mile main road curves left and side road goes straight. Curve left for 0.4 mile to Point Judith Coast Guard Station, at end. Leave your bike outside the gate to the station (and lock it), and enjoy the views from the grounds on foot. The "No Vehicles" sign at the gate is taken literally by Coast Guard personnel.
- Backtrack a half mile to Pilgrim Avenue on right.
- Right for 0.2 mile to Calef Avenue.
- Left along ocean for 0.4 mile to end (Ocean Road).
- Right for 4.8 miles to end, at traffic light just past Towers. If you bear right on Newton Avenue just after Ocean Road curves sharply right, there is a spectacular view of rocky shoreline. Another small road, 0.3 mile after Newton Avenue, leads to another fine ocean view.
- Bear right for one block to another light (Narragansett Avenue on left). Here the short ride turns left.
- Straight for 1.2 miles to small road on right immediately after Narrow River bridge. Follow it for a half mile to Route 1A.
- Cross Route 1A diagonally onto Old Boston Neck Road. Go 0.3 mile to Middlebridge Road on left.
- Left for one mile to Torry Road on left.
- Left for a half mile to end (Route 1). Hill!
- Turn right. Just ahead make U-turn at traffic light, using ramp to cross highway at right angles. Go 0.2 mile to Saugatucket Road on right, at traffic light.
- Right for 5 miles to end (Route 110), going straight at three crossroads.
- Left for 1.3 miles to crossroads (Tuckertown Road on left).

- Left for 2.4 miles to end
- Left for 1.4 miles traffic light (Stedman's Bicycle Shop on right at corner); right on Woodruff Avenue for 1.1 miles to shopping center on right.

Directions for the ride: 16 miles

- Follow first 10 directions of long ride to Narragansett Avenue on left, at traffic light.
- Left for 0.1 mile to another light (Route 1A on right).
- Right for 1.1 mile to Lambert Street on left, immediately after red-brick church on right. (Indian statue on right after 0.1 mile at traffic light; South County Museum after 0.4 mile on Strathmore Road on right).
- Left on Lambert Street for 0.3 mile to end. Right and immediate left on Route 108; shopping center on right.

hot weekend afternoons, and elegant cedar-shingled homes over-looking the sea. Short dead-end roads afford even better views of the rocky coast.

You continue on through the pleasant seaside community of Narragansett Pier and under the stone arch of the Towers. Just ahead the short ride turns inland and passes another landmark, a magnificent wooden sculpture of a Narragansett Indian chief. If you turn right after the statue on Strathmore Road, you'll come to the South County Museum, with exhibits of early Rhode Island rural life and industries.

The long ride continues north to the Narrow River (also called the Pettaquamscutt River), a slender saltwater inlet paralleling the coastline which you'll cross twice on picturesque bridges, first on Route 1A and then on Middlebridge Road. The one tough climb of the ride awaits you when you turn inland from the riverbank. The rest of the tour passes through a typical South County landscape of fine homes, woodlots, little ponds, and small farms bordered by stone walls and shade trees.

26. Block Island

Number of miles: 16

Terrain: Delightfully rolling, with lots of little ups and downs, and a nice downhill run at the end.

Start: Ferry dock at Old Harbor, in the center of town. The ferries from Galilee, Providence, Newport, and New London, Connecticut, land here. (The ferry from Montauk, Long Island, lands at New Harbor, a mile west of Old Harbor).

Food: Grocery store and snack bar in town.

Caution: Block Island has a unique hazard—mopeds, which are rented by the hundreds during the summer with no instruction on how to operate them safely. Mopeds frequently stop dead in the middle of the road without warning. I've also seen moped riders wobbling along with one arm full of parcels and overloaded wire baskets spilling their contents into the road.

Block Island offers 16 miles of some of the most delightful cycling and scenery in the state. The teardrop-shaped island, about ten miles out to sea, is five miles long and three miles across at its widest point. The northern half is dominated by Great Salt Pond, which extends across the entire width of the island except for a narrow strip.

The Block Island landscape is unlike anything else in the state. The island is treeless, containing a unique scrubby, moorland vegetation which rises and falls in an endless series of small bubble-like hills and hollows. On the southeastern shore are the magnificient Mohegan Bluffs, rising over a hundred feet nearly straight up from the sea and carved by erosion into jagged formations.

The boat from Galilee lands in town, a picturesque mixture of rambling Victorian hotels and trim wooden homes. Just out of town is the fine public beach, then head to the northern tip, where a dirt path leads nearly a mile to the abandoned North Lighthouse, standing in bleak, total isolation amidst an eerie landscape of sand dunes and sea.

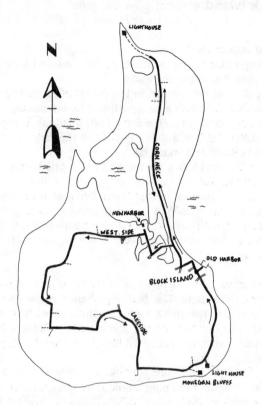

How to get there: To get to Galilee, exit south from Route 1 onto Route 108. Go about four miles to the road to Galilee on right. Follow this road to end and turn left. Ferry dock is just ahead. The Providence ferry dock is on India Street at the head of the harbor. From Route 195 (the section east of I-95), take the Gano Street exit and turn left at the end of the exit ramp. Go to end, just ahead, and turn right on India Street. The dock is a half mile ahead on left, next to a nightclub. For schedules, call the Block Island Boat, 783-4613, or AAA.

Directions for the ride

- Right at end of dock entrance. Just ahead road turns 90 degrees left. Go 0.1 mile to crossroads (Corn Neck Road).
- Right for 3.7 miles to end. From here a dirt path leads 0.7 mile to North Lighthouse and another 0.3 mile to Sandy Point, the extreme tip.
- Backtrack for 3.3 miles to first main road on right, Beach Avenue. It crosses small bridge.
- Right for 0.4 mile to first right, Ocean Avenue.
- Right for 0.3 mile to West Side Road on left. New Harbor dock is straight ahead.
- Left for 0.2 mile to fork, and bear right for 3.8 miles to end (merge right at stop sign).
- Bear right on Lakeside Drive. After one mile road curves 90 degrees left onto Mohegan Trail. Continue for 0.9 mile to a dirt path, which bears to the right, leading to Mohegan Bluffs. It's shortly before the red-brick Southeast Lighthouse.
- Continue on main road for a quarter mile to another dirt path on right that leads to bicycle racks. The main viewing area for the bluffs is 100 yards beyond the racks. A stairway leads down to the beach.
- Leaving Bluffs, turn right for 1.6 miles to crossroads and stop sign at bottom of hill.
- Bear left to dock, just ahead on right.

After returning toward town, circle the wide southern half of the island on roads winding through the moors, with views of the ocean around every curve. The architectural styles of the summer homes vary widely, from traditional cedar-shingled, peaked-roof cottages to bold ultramodern structures with sharp angles that seem even sharper against the stark, treeless landscape. Unfortunately, the island is undergoing a building boom which, let's hope, will be controlled or regulated before the unspoiled appearance of the land is destroyed. Near the end of the ride, from the top of Mohegan Bluffs, you'll gaze in wonder at one of the most spectacular views in Rhode Island.

A trip to Block Island should be an unhurried, leisurely experience. Take an early boat and spend the day or even a weekend poking around the numerous dirt roads leading down to the ocean or to the Coast Guard Station on Great Salt Pond. You can easily spend a couple hours exploring Mohegan Bluffs alone. When you get back to town, browse through the colorful gift and antique shops or relax at the beach. If it's a warm, clear day, treat yourself to the four-hour ferry trip from Providence, which follows the entire length of Narragansett Bay and stops at Newport before continuing on to Block Island. You'll have less time to explore the island unless you stay overnight, but the delightful trip along the bay will more than make up for it. If you stay overnight, be sure to make reservations in advance. Camping is not permitted.

27. Pedaler's Paradise: Jamestown

Number of miles: 16 (25 with Fort Getty-Beavertail extension)
Terrain: Rolling, with one short steep hill. The long ride has an additional hill at the beginning of Beavertail Road.
Start: The island side of the Jamestown Bridge, Route 138. Park on south side of road. If a new bridge is built, park at the end of the old bridge.
Food: Grocery store and snack bar in town opposite the harbor.

The island of Jamestown, which guards the mouth of Narragansett Bay between Newport and the mainland, is a most enjoyable spot for bicycling. As you pedal around the slender island, less than two miles across at its widest point, views of the bay emerge around every bend. Because Jamestown's population is small, traffic on the side roads is very light. The only heavily traveled road is Route 138, the artery between the mainland and Newport, which you will ride along only briefly.

From the bridge, head inland to the center of the island, and turn south at the bottom of a sharp hill on North Main Road. At the top of a gradual rise, there is an old windmill on your left, dating from 1787. Restored to operating condition by the Jamestown Historical Society, it is open to visitors on weekend afternoons. Continue south, descending to a salt marsh and then climbing another gradual hill to the intersection with Narragansett Avenue, which heads toward the center of town. Here the ride goes straight ahead, but if you turn left you can visit the Jamestown Museum, a nineteenth-century schoolhouse with memorabilia from the old ferries (pre-dating the bridges) and other items of local interest. Also on Narragansett Avenue is the Fire Department Memorial Building, with a collection of antique firefighting equipment.

The short ride now continues on Highland Drive, along the southern shore of the main part of the island. This narrow, curving lane bobs up and down little hills, passing rambling cedar-shingled homes with gables and turrets overlooking the rocky ledges along the shore. Just ahead is Fort Wetherill State Park, a magnificent spot

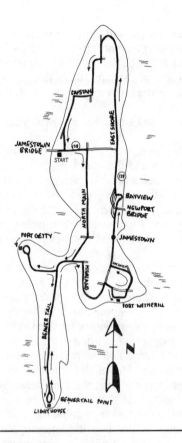

How to get there: From the north, head south on I-95 and Routes 4 and 1 to Route 138 East. Go east on Route 138 for 3 miles to bridge. From the south, exit east from I-95 onto Route 138, and follow it to bridge. From the east, head south on Route 24 until it joins Route 138. Exit south on Route 138 and follow it across the Newport Bridge to the beginning of the Jamestown Bridge.

Directions for the ride: 25 miles

- Head away from bridge on Route 138 for 0.8 mile to traffic light at bottom of hill. Go right for 2.1 miles to traffic light (Narragansett Avenue).
- Straight for 0.6 mile to where you merge with a road coming in on the left at a sharp angle (Hamilton Avenue). Here the short ride turns sharp left.
- Bear right for 0.4 mile to first right (Fort Getty Road).
- Right for one mile to tip of peninsula. Make a small counterclockwise loop and return along the same road to end (Beavertail Road).
- Right for 2.8 miles to fork, just before lighthouse at tip of Beavertail Point. (Note: A bike path is planned for Beavertail Point State Park. If one is built, use it instead of the road to go to the lighthouse. When you leave the park, you will return along Beavertail Road, the same road which leads to it.)
- Bear right at fork, go past lighthouse, and continue for 0.6 mile to fork.
- Bear right out of park on Beavertail Road for 2.7 miles to fork just past causeway. Go straight (don't bear left) for 100 yards to Highland Drive.
- Right for 1.4 miles to crossroads at small traffic island (Blueberry Lane on left).
- Turn right and immediately bear right at stop sign. Go 0.2 mile to entrance to Fort Wetherill State Park, on right.
- Right into park, and explore it on one-way loops. Leave park at entrance 0.2 mile east of first one, at bottom of hill.
- Left out of park and immediately right on Racquet Road. Go 0.3 mile to fork. Bear left for 0.3 mile to end, at top of hill. (**Caution:** Beginning of this stretch is very bumpy and gravelly. It is safest to walk your bike.)
- Right for 1.1 mile to fork where main road bears left and Bayview Drive bears right.
- Bear right for 0.8 mile to end (Route 138).
- Right for 1.2 miles to where Route 138 turns left.
- Straight on East Shore Road for 3.8 miles to crossroads and stop sign (dirt road straight). **Caution:** Last half mile is bumpy.

- Right for 1.3 miles to Capstan Street (unmarked) on right, mid-way up hill (next right after West Reach Road).
- Turn right. After a half mile road turns 90 degrees left at water. Go one mile to fork (**Caution:** Steep downhill just before turn.)
- Bear left at fork on Beach Avenue for a half mile to Route 138.
- Turn right. Starting point is just ahead.

Directions for the ride: 16 miles

- Follow first 2 directions of long ride.
- Sharp left on Hamilton Avenue for 100 yards to Highland Drive on right.
- Follow last 12 directions of long ride, beginning "Right for 1.4 miles to crossroads . . ."

worth exploring. The fort, built between 1899 and 1906, is a massive structure on a cliff overlooking the bay, complete with turrets, ramparts, underground ammunition rooms, and mysterious narrow tunnels. The complex housed hundreds of troops during the two World Wars. Next to the fort are little roads looping around the adjoining cliffs.

Head north along the eastern side of the island, passing Jamestown Harbor and pedaling underneath the Newport Bridge. As you bike along the northern half of the island, which is less developed than the southern half, the road ascends onto low ridges, with fields and gentleman farms sloping to the bay a couple of hundred yards away. As you curve south for the return leg, you go inland through a wooded area, and then descend sharply to the western shore. The final portion of the ride hugs the shoreline, with the graceful arch of the Jamestown Bridge always in view.

The long ride includes the narrow peninsula that extends to the southwest below the main part of the island. First head toward Fort Getty, a small headland on the west shore with some old fortifications and a campground. Then proceed south to Beavertail Point at the tip of the peninsula. The point, a state park, is a spectacular rocky promontory with a granite lighthouse built in 1856. On windy days, the surf crashes onto the rocks with an awe-inspiring display of natural forces. The state recently acquired over 150 acres of surplus Navy property, greatly enlarging the park. The park soon will include a bicycle path around its perimeter. Return to the main part of the island, passing through open fields and moors. Just past the causeway along Mackerel Cove, between the Beavertail peninsula and the main island, you rejoin the long ride on Highland Drive.

28. Barrington Ride

Number of miles: 13
Terrain: Flat.
Start: Commuter parking lot, Routes 114 and 103, Barrington.
Food: Newport Creamery and Friendly's on County Road.

On this ride, one of the flattest and most relaxing in the book, you'll explore Barrington, a well-to-do suburb of Providence on the eastern shore of Narragansett Bay. The ride abounds with tranquil runs along the water and goes past Barrington Beach, a good spot for a swim on a hot day. The last part of the ride follows a recently completed section of the lovely East Bay Bicycle Path.

The ride starts behind the stately white church overlooking the Barrington River. Cross the bridge and enjoy a lovely run along the river. Cross the river again and continue to follow it on Mathewson Road, an idyllic lane from which you can see the church spires and picturesque old wharves of the town of Warren.

Turn westward toward Narragansett Bay. Barrington Beach, tucked away at the end of a side street, is a pleasant spot for a rest. Just ahead, pedal through the Rhode Island Country Club, with lush green fairways sloping gently from the road to the bay. At Nayatt Point, gracious homes with beautifully landscaped grounds keep watch along the shore.

The route turns inland briefly to go alongside unspoiled Echo Lake, then dips down to the bay once again. Go around Allens Neck, where you have fine views of the water. Just ahead is Haines Memorial State Park, a pleasant picnic spot that extends down to Bullocks Cove, an inlet of the bay. Near the end of the ride, pedal for about three miles along a newly constructed portion of the East Bay Bicycle Path, which hugs the shore of Brickyard Pond. When completed, the path will run from the Providence waterfront to Bristol. In the center of town, you will see the elegant stone town hall, built in 1888, on Route 103.

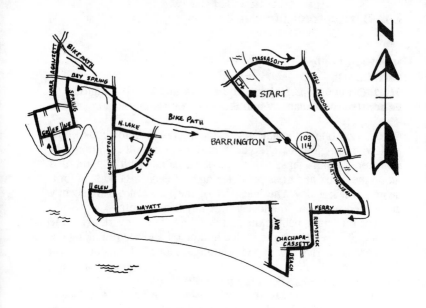

How to get there: From the north, exit south from Route 195 onto Route 114. Go about 5½ miles to traffic light with big white church on far left corner. Parking lot is on left just after church. From the east, exit west from Route 195 onto Route 103, toward Warren. Go about 6 miles to Route 114 in downtown Warren. Right for about 2½ miles to parking lot on right, just before church. By bike from Providence, head east on Waterman Street. Right on Gano Street. Climb stairs on right to Route 195 overpass. Cross Seekonk River bridge on sidewalk. Jog right and immediately left along river on First Avenue and Veterans Memorial Parkway. Go about 3.5 miles to Willett Avenue (Route 103) on left, at traffic light. Follow Route 103 for about 4 miles to traffic light with big white church on far left corner. Parking lot is just past light on left.

Directions for the ride:

- Right out of parking lot to traffic light just ahead.
- Right on Massasoit Avenue for 0.8 mile to end.
- Right for 1.3 miles to end (County Road, Route 103).
- Right for 0.2 mile to Mathewson Road, immediately after bridge.
- Turn left. After 0.8 miles road turns 90 degrees right. Continue 0.7 mile to end (Rumstick Road).
- Left for 0.3 mile to where main road curves sharply right and small road goes straight.
- Curve right. Just ahead, go straight on Chachapacassett Road for 0.3 mile to Beach Road, at bottom of hill.
- Left for 0.1 mile to water. Walk bike around barricade and turn right along water (Barrington Beach) for one block.
- Bear right uphill on Bay Street for 0.4 mile to end (Nayatt Road).
- Left for 1.3 miles to where the main road turns right on Washington Road and a smaller road goes straight.
- Straight for 0.1 mile to fork. Bear right 0.2 mile to Glen Avenue.
- Right for 0.2 mile to end (Washington Road).
- Left for 0.1 mile to narrow lane on right immediately after bridge.
- Right for a half mile to crossroads (North Lake Drive).
- Left for 0.4 mile to end (Washington Road).
- Right for 0.6 mile to Bay Spring Street.
- Left for 0.4 mile to Spring Avenue, opposite lace mill.
- Left for 0.3 mile to end (Greene Avenue).
- Right for one short block to crossroads.
- Left for 0.2 mile to crossroads (Greene Avenue again).
- Left for one short block to end (Shore Drive).
- Right for one block to end (Latham Avenue).
- Right for 0.1 mile to crossroads (Narragansett Avenue).
- Left for 0.4 mile to East Bay Bicycle Path. Haines Memorial State Park on right.
- Right on bike path for 2.8 miles to County Road (Route 103). Shopping center on right at intersection.
- Left on County Road for 1 mile to parking lot on right. Historic town hall on right after 0.2 mile.

29. Bristol—Portsmouth

Number of miles: 15 (25 with Portsmouth loop)

Terrain: Flat, with two short hills. The long ride has a tough climb up to and then over the Mount Hope Bridge.

Start: Newport Creamery, corner of Route 114 and Gooding Avenue, Bristol.

Food: Several grocery stores and snack bars en route. Newport Creamery at end.

Tolls: 30¢ each way over the Mount Hope Bridge on the long ride.

Fine views of Narragansett and Mount Hope Bays abound on this flat, scenic ride. The historic town of Bristol commands a peninsula poised between Narragansett Bay on the west and Mount Hope Bay on the east. A highlight of the ride is a run along the bike path through Colt State Park, a magnificent, well-maintained former estate with an extensive waterfront on Narragansett Bay. The park was originally owned by Samuel P. Colt, nephew of the inventor of the Colt revolver.

The beginning of the ride goes through the park. The entrance road, a divided parkway with a column of trees down the middle, slopes along a grassy hillside with the bay glistening in the distance. Just ahead turn onto the bike path, which meanders past a salt marsh, over a picturesque stone-arched bridge, and along the bay. Pass the handsome stone main mansion (built as a barn), guarded by two bronze lions. Just ahead is the Coggeshall Farm Museum, a working restoration of an eighteenth-century farm with barnyard animals, an herb garden, and craft demonstrations.

Beyond the park, the road winds along the head of Bristol Harbor. A mile later go through the center of town, passing the elegant marble Colt Memorial, now an elementary school. On the next block are two Federal-style mansions and a handsome stone church built in 1860. Just ahead is Saint Michael's Chapel, dating from 1876.

South of downtown, follow the harbor to the tip of the penin-

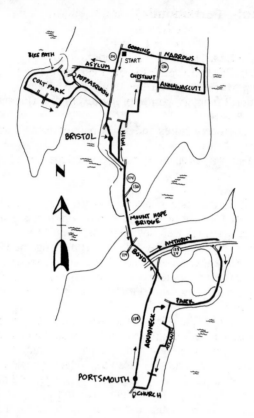

How to get there: From the north, exit south from Route 195 onto Route 114 for about 10 miles to parking lot on left, immediately after traffic light. From the east, exit from Route 195 onto Route 103, heading toward Warren. In Warren, turn left on Route 136 and go about three miles to traffic light (Narrows Road on left, Gooding Avenue on right). Right to parking lot on left, at end. By bike from Providence, go to start of Barrington ride (Ride 28). Continue on Route 114 for about 5 miles to parking lot on left, just past Gooding Avenue traffic light.

Directions for the ride: 25 miles

- Left out of parking lot on Route 114 for 0.3 mile to Colt State Park entrance road on right, at traffic light.
- Right for a half mile to where main road bears left and side road goes straight. (Side road leads to beach.)
- Bear left for 0.2 mile to rotary.
- Go two-thirds around rotary to second right, and proceed 0.1 mile to bike path.
- Right for 1.1 mile to stone bridge. Continue 0.2 mile to another bike path on right. (**Caution:** Watch for pedestrians, joggers, dogs, and horses.)
- Right for a quarter mile to automobile road, and straight for 100 yards to bike path along bay.
- Left for 0.7 mile to automobile road, just after you curve left away from water.
- Cross automobile road and go 0.2 mile to where bike path turns 90 degrees left and grassy path goes straight.
- Walk bike along grassy path (stone mansion on left). After 100 yards, continue straight on paved road for 0.4 mile to end (Poppasquash Road).
- Left for 1.2 miles to end (Route 114). Go right for 0.2 mile to fork.
- Bear left (still Route 114) for 2.4 miles to Mount Hope Bridge toll booth. Here the short ride makes a U-turn. (**Caution:** Watch for car doors opening into your path in downtown area. If you want a look at the buildings, it's safest to walk your bike a few blocks.) (Nice view from behind Saint Columban's Seminary, after 1.9 miles.)
- Cross bridge to fork at far end (Route 114 bears right). (**Caution:** It's safest to walk your bike across the expansion joints.)
- Bear left for 0.4 mile to Anthony Road on left, at bottom of hill (sign says Common Fence Point).
- Left for 1.5 miles to fork just after going under Routes 24 and 138 (sign points left to Island Park).
- Bear left for 2 miles to Aquidneck Avenue on left, just as you start to go uphill. Go left for 0.2 mile to end (Atlantic Avenue).
- Turn left. After 1.1 mile, main road curves 90 degrees right uphill. Continue 0.2 mile to end (Route 138).

- Right for 1.6 miles to traffic light at bottom of hill (Boyd Lane). (**Caution:** Route 138 is very busy four-lane road with no shoulder. Ride in middle of right lane rather than at edge.)
- Bear left for 0.7 mile to end. Bear right across bridge. At toll booth, continue 0.3 mile to fork (Route 114 bears left, Route 136 bears right).
- Bear left for 0.7 mile to where Route 114 curves left; curve left for 0.2 mile to High Street.
- Bear right for 1.1 miles to end (Washington Street).
- Right for 0.1 mile to end.
- Turn left. After 0.4 mile, road turns 90 degrees left at top of hill. Continue a half mile to end (Chestnut Street). Right for 0.4 mile to end (route 136).
- Jog right and immediately left on Annawamscutt Road. (**Caution:** Watch for traffic.) Go 0.9 mile to bay.
- Left just before water for a half mile to end (Narrows Road).
- Left for 0.9 mile to traffic light (Route 136).
- Straight for 0.8 mile to parking lot on left.

Directions for the ride: 15 miles

- Follow long ride to Mount Hope Bridge toll booth.
- Make a U-turn and go 0.3 mile to fork (Route 114 bears left, Route 136 bears right).
- Follow last 8 directions of long ride.

sula. You pass Blithewold, a Newport-style mansion with extensive landscaped grounds and gardens sweeping down to the bay. It was formerly the summer residence of Augustus VanWickle, a Pennsylvania coal magnate. Just ahead is the idyllic Saint Columban's Seminary, on a grassy hillside sloping to the shore. A road looping behind the seminary provides a magnificent view. At the tip of the peninsula, the bold, modern campus of Roger Williams College stands guard above Mount Hope Bay.

The short ride returns through town along High Street, which is graced by several elegant homes originally owned by sea captains, and an impressive cluster of nineteenth-century schools and churches. To finish the ride, climb the ridge forming the spine of the peninsula and enjoy a gentle descent to the shore of Mount Hope Bay. Hug the shoreline on a quiet residential street, then turn west back to the starting point.

The long ride leaves Bristol to cross the spectacular, mile-long Mount Hope Bridge to Portsmouth. On a clear day, the view from the top is unparalleled, and you should walk some of the way to fully savor it. In Portsmouth, ride along the broad Sakonnet River for several miles, passing the remains of the stone bridge that used to span the narrowest point between Portsmouth and Tiverton. The center span of the bridge collapsed during the 1938 hurricane and was replaced by the Sakonnet Bridge, a mile to the north. Head back to the Mount Hope Bridge through the center of town to rejoin the short ride.

From Bristol Harbor you can take the ferry to Prudence Island in the middle of Narragansett Bay. This is a peaceful spot with some summer homes and large expanses of undeveloped woodland, roamed by deer, at the north and south ends. For information on ferry schedules call Prudence Island Navigation Company, 245-7411.

30. Portsmouth—Middletown: Aquidneck Island North

Number of miles: 19 (24 with Saint George's School–Second Beach extension)

Terrain: Gently rolling, with a tough hill at the beginning, and an additional short, steep climb.

Start: IGA Supermarket, Route 138, Portsmouth.

Food: Grocery stores and snack bars on Route 138 at end.

Caution: The ride has some stretches on Route 138, a busy, undivided four-lane highway with no shoulders. It's safer to bike in the middle of the right lane rather than at the edge, forcing traffic coming up behind you to pass you in the left lane, rather than brushing past you by inches.

Aquidneck Island, which is officially the island of Rhode Island, contains the communities of Portsmouth in the north, Middletown in the middle, and Newport in the south. Long and slender, the island is 15 miles long from tip to tip, and five miles across at its widest point. Magnificently situated in the center of Narragansett Bay, with broad stretches of open farmland sloping gently down to the shore, Aquidneck Island contains some of the finest biking territory in the state.

From the ride's beginning in the center of Portsmouth, there's an immediate long climb to the top of the ridge that forms a spine down the middle of the island. You ride along the ridge looking down on broad expanses of open land. Then coast down a long hill to the shore of the bay, passing some Navy housing. At the bottom, just off the route, is a marina, restaurant, and dock for the ferry to Prudence Island, all on former Navy property.

This ride turns sharply left on Burma Road, a lightly travelled road hugging the bay for several miles on deactivated Navy property. This is one of the most enjoyable runs in the state. Toward the end of Burma Road, you'll see the huge docks of the Naval Surface Force of the United States Atlantic Fleet. Destroyers and other enormous ships are usually at anchor alongside the docks. Opposite the last dock turn inland up a short hill, passing the headquarters

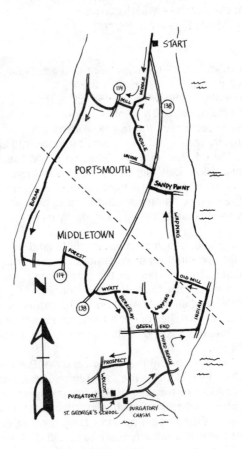

How to get there: From the north and east, exit south from Route 195 onto Route 24. Take the third exit after the Sakonnet Bridge (Turnpike Avenue, To Route 138). At end of ramp go 0.8 mile to end (Route 138). Bear right, and IGA is just ahead on left. From the west, cross the Newport Bridge and head north on Route 138 for about 8 miles to IGA on right, at bottom of long hill.

Directions for the ride: 24 miles

- Left out of parking lot for a half mile to where Route 138 curves left and Middle Road goes straight, almost at top of hill.
- Straight for 1 mile to Mill Lane.
- Right for 0.6 mile to end (Route 114). (**Caution:** End comes up suddenly at bottom of steep hill. Test brakes in advance.)
- Left for 0.1 mile to first right (sign says Melville).
- Right for 0.8 mile almost to bottom of hill, to where you merge with a road coming in on left at a sharp angle (Burma Road).
- Sharp left for 4.4 miles to a road that bears left uphill, opposite destroyer dock; sign may say NETC, Gate 11. (**Caution:** Bad diagonal railroad tracks 0.7 mile before intersection.)
- Bear left for 0.8 mile to end (Route 114).
- Left for 0.2 mile to Forest Avenue. (**Caution:** Route 114 is extremely busy. Safest to use sidewalk for this brief stretch.)
- Right for 0.9 mile to end (Route 138). Left for 0.2 mile to second right (Wyatt Road).
- Right for 0.3 mile to crossroads (Turner Road).
- Straight for 0.2 mile to Berkeley Avenue on right. Here the short ride goes straight.
- Right for 0.9 mile to crossroads (Green End Avenue). Continue straight for a half mile to Prospect Avenue. Right for 0.6 mile to end.
- Turn left, and then immediately bear left on Wolcott Avenue for 0.7 mile to crossroads (Purgatory Road).
- Left for a half mile to fork at bottom of hill (Paradise Road bears left). Saint George's School is on left at top of hill. Purgatory Chasm is 100 yards off route on Tuckerman Avenue.
- Bear right for 0.4 mile to another fork.
- Bear left, passing Hanging Rock, for 0.8 mile to crossroads (Third Beach Road).
- Left for one mile to crossroads (Green End Avenue).
- Right for 0.8 mile to end (Indian Avenue).
- Left for 0.8 mile to Old Mill Lane. Left for 0.7 mile to end (Wapping Road).
- Right for 1.9 miles to end (Sandy Point Road).
- Left for a half mile to end (Route 138).

- Right for a half mile to Union Street on left, immediately after state police station. Glen Estate on right.
- Left for 0.1 mile to Middle Road. **Extreme caution** turning left onto Union Street.
- Right for one mile to stop sign; bear left (still Middle Road) for 0.6 mile to fork. Bear left (still Middle Road) for 0.8 mile to end.
- Bear left into Route 138 for a half mile to IGA on right, at bottom of hill.

Directions for the ride: 19 miles

- Follow first 11 directions of long ride, to corner of Wyatt Road and Berkeley Avenue.
- Straight for 0.6 mile to end (Mitchells Lane).
- Right for a half mile to fork.
- Bear left on Wapping Road for 2.9 miles to end (Sandy Point Road).
- Follow last 5 directions of long ride.

of the Naval Underwater Systems Center, which conducts highly technical research for the Navy.

After heading inland for a couple of miles, the long ride turns south on Berkeley Avenue, which runs past large, prosperous farms bordered by trim stone walls. You pass Whitehall, a colonial mansion built in 1729 by George Berkeley, the philosopher and educator. At Prospect Avenue there's a well-maintained country schoolhouse with a graceful cupola. Two miles beyond is Saint George's School, a prestigious preparatory school crowning a hilltop, with its English Gothic stone chapel. The vaulted interior of the chapel, a masterpiece of design reminiscent of European cathedrals, is worth a visit.

Just past Saint George's, only a hundred yards off the route, is Purgatory Chasm, a narrow cleft in the cliffs along the ocean. You continue past undeveloped Second Beach and Hanging Rock, a massive boulder perched ominously above the road. If you pedal furiously you can probably get beyond it before it topples. A mile farther is the tranquil Norman Audubon Sanctuary.

After a long, sweeping downhill run, you follow the bay northward for several miles, closely at first, and then about a half mile inland through beautiful, well-manicured estates. You will pass the extensive grounds of the Glen Estate, which is the major center for horse jumping in New England. To finish the ride, follow the island's center ridge on Middle Road, and swoop down the same long hill that you struggled up at the beginning.

The short ride bypasses Saint George's School and Second Beach by heading east directly toward the bay instead of turning south on Berkeley Avenue. You traverse acres of open farmland, and enjoy a long downhill run on Wapping Road with views of the bay in the distance. At the bottom, you rejoin the long ride two miles before the Glen Estate.

31. Middletown—Portsmouth:
Aquidneck Island Central

Number of miles: 17
Terrain: Gently rolling, with one hill on Third Beach Road.
Start: Portsmouth Middle School, Jepson Lane in Portsmouth,
Rhode Island.
Food: None en route.
Caution: This ride has two sections on Route 138, a busy,
undivided four-lane highway with no shoulders. Ride in the
middle of the right lane rather than at the edge so that traffic
must pass you in the left lane.

Aquidneck Island contains such fine biking territory that I've included a second ride through Middletown and Portsmouth. This
ride starts from about halfway down the island, just north of the
Portsmouth-Middletown line. Begin by pedaling south along Jepson
Lane, where broad expanses of open land stretch for acres on both
sides of the road. On your left you can see Sisson Pond, a couple
hundred yards off the road. Occasional new homes, stark-looking
against the treeless landscape, dot the roadside. As the population
of the island grows, due primarily to expanding high-tech industries
like Raytheon and the Naval Underwater Systems Center, more and
more new houses are going up on what was once unspoiled farmland. Fortunately, most of the island is still undeveloped.

As you head south on Berkeley Avenue and Paradise Road, the
landscape becomes more gracious in appearance, with gentleman
farms bordered by orderly, squared-off stone walls and gateposts.
You'll pass Whitehall, the 1729 mansion of philosopher and educator George Berkeley. Dominating the horizon ahead of you is the
Gothic spire of the Saint George's School Chapel, which is worth
visiting. If you'd like to see it, bear right instead of left at the end of
Paradise Road, curve right while going up the hill, and turn right
into the school at the top.

Paradise Road leads all the way down to the ocean at Second
Beach, which is refreshingly undeveloped and uncommercialized.

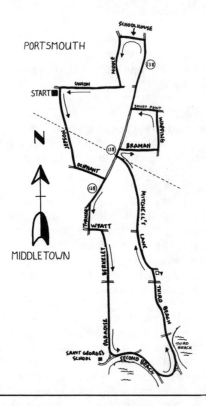

How to get there: From the north, take Route 114 south to Union Street on left. It's three miles south of the end of Route 24, or six miles south of the Mount Hope Bridge. Turn left at traffic light on Union Street and take first right on Jepson Lane. The school is just ahead on the right. From the south, cross the Newport Bridge and exit north on Route 138. Go half mile to Route 114 and the traffic light. Turn left on Route 114 and go about four miles to Union Street, on the right. Turn right on Union Street and take your first right on Jepson Lane. The school is just ahead on the right.

Directions for the ride:

- Right out of parking lot for 1.3 miles to end (Oliphant Lane). Go left for a half mile to end (Route 138), then right for a half mile to Turner Road.

- Bear left for 0.3 mile to crossroads (Wyatt Road). Go left for 0.2 mile to Berkeley Avenue, then right for 0.9 mile to crossroads (Green End Avenue). Continue straight for 1.3 miles to fork at bottom of hill.

- Bear left for 100 yards to end, and bear left again for 0.3 mile to fork.

- Bear right for 0.4 mile to another fork. Bear left on smaller road for 0.2 mile to another fork (bumpy, rutted road bears right).

- Bear left for a half mile to crossroads (Indian Avenue). (**Caution:** Just after you bear left there's a bad speed bump and a deep sand patch.)

- Straight for one mile to crossroads (Green End Avenue). Continue straight for 0.3 mile to where Mitchells Lane bears left. Bear left for a half mile to where Mitchells Lane bears right. Bear right for 1.3 miles to end (Route 138).

- Right for 100 yards to Bramans Lane. Go right for 0.9 mile to end (Wapping Road).

- Left for one mile to end (Sandy Point Road). Left for a half mile to end (Route 138).

- Right for 1.6 miles to Schoolhouse Lane on left, just past house number 1443 on right.

- Left for 0.4 mile to Middle Road. (**Caution** making this turn.)

- Left for one mile to end (Union Street).

- Right for 1.4 miles to Jepson Lane, shortly before traffic light. Left for 0.2 mile to school on right.

Bike along the beach and cross the narrow neck to Third Beach. Between the two beaches, at the southeast corner of the island, lies Sachuest Point, an unspoiled sandy peninsula that recently became a National Wildlife Reserve. If you'd like to visit it, bear right instead of left at the end of Second Beach, adding about two and a half miles to the ride.

Head north along Third Beach, and just ahead pass the Norman Audubon Sanctuary, a lovely expanse of fields and woodland. As you proceed on Route 138, an inspiring vista of the water, a mile away across the meadows, extends before you. To finish the ride, head west across the island on Union Street, which runs alongside Saint Mary's Pond.

32. Newport—Middletown: Aquidneck Island South

Number of miles: 18 (25 with Middletown extension)
Terrain: Flat, with one hill on the longer ride.
Start: Zayre's parking lot, corner of Route 114 and Chases Lane in Middletown, Rhode Island. The parking lot is immediately south of the Newport Motor Inn on the right.
Food: Lum's, Route 114, just north of the starting point. McDonald's, Route 114, about a mile south of the starting point.
Caution: On summer weekends, traffic along the harbor, Ocean Drive, and the mansion area is very heavy. The best time to bike during the summer is early morning.

Newport is the scenic, historic, and architectural pinnacle of Rhode Island. The city contains mansions of incredible opulence once owned by Vanderbilts and Astors, and narrow streets lined with historic homes and public buildings. The bustling waterfront is complete with boutiques, haute-cuisine restaurants, and docks with sleek yachts moored beside them. For several miles, magnificent Ocean Drive runs along the rocky shoreline passing mansion after mansion. Many mansions offer guided tours to the public, and most are located on Bellevue Avenue. The largest and most ornate mansion of all is The Breakers on Ochre Point Avenue, formerly owned by the Vanderbilts. Rosecliff, not far behind in opulence, was the setting for part of the movie, "The Great Gatsby."

The ride starts by skirting the Newport Naval Base, one of the largest in the country until it was deactivated several years ago. You pass under the Newport Bridge, one of the longest and most impressive on the East Coast; unfortunately bikes are not allowed on the bridge itself, because of wheel-eating expansion joints. Go along the harbor, lined with hundreds of boats and yachts, and pass Fort Adams State Park, with its massive fortification overlooking Newport Harbor. Just past Fort Adams is Hammersmith Farm, an estate formerly owned by the Auchincloss family, the parents of Jacqueline Kennedy Onassis, and now open to the public. John F.

MIDDLETOWN

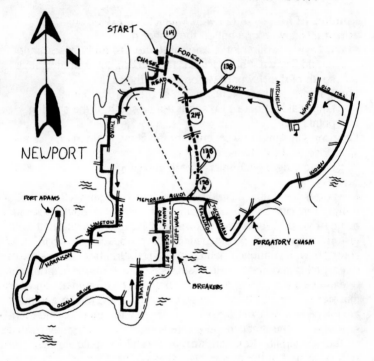

NEWPORT

How to get there: From the Providence area, head east on Route 195 and exit south on Route 24 to end (Route 114). Straight for about 6 miles to parking lot on right, just past Newport Motor Inn. From Taunton area and north, head south on Route 24 to end (Route 114). Proceed as above. From the east, head west on Route 195 and exit south on Route 24 to end (Route 114). Proceed as above. From the west, head east on Route 138 to fork where Route 138 bears right and Route 114 goes straight. Straight for 0.7 mile to parking lot on left.

Directions for the ride: 25 miles

- Right out of side of parking lot on Chases Lane (not Route 114) to first left (Read Street).
- Left for 0.3 mile to end (Jones Street). Left for 0.2 mile to end (Coddington Highway). Right for 0.6 mile to fork (main road bears left).
- Bear left for 0.7 mile to rotary. Right for 0.1 mile to first left, at traffic light (Third Street).
- Left for a half mile to Sycamore Street on right, immediately after you go under Newport Bridge.
- Right for 0.9 mile to end (America's Cup Avenue), passing bridge to Goat Island and Sheraton Hotel.
- Right for 0.4 mile to Thames Street, at traffic light (post office on far left corner). Docks are worth exploring.
- Right along harbor for a half mile to Wellington Avenue, at traffic island.
- Right for 0.8 mile to crossroads (Harrison Avenue). Right for 0.4 mile to end.
- Right for a half mile to entrance road to Fort Adams (worth visiting).
- Straight for 0.4 mile to fork. Bear right on Ridge Road for 4.6 miles to end. Ridge Road becomes Ocean Drive.
- Turn right. Just ahead road turns 90 degrees left on Bellevue Avenue. Go 1.3 miles to small crossroads just past Rosecliff (Ruggles Avenue).
- Right for 0.4 mile to Ochre Point Avenue on left. If you wish, continue to end (nice view), left on the Cliff Walk, and *walk* your bike a half mile to end (Memorial Boulevard). Resume ride there (2 directions ahead).
- Left on Ochre Point Avenue for a half mile to end, passing The Breakers. Go left for 0.1 mile to first right (Annandale Road). Right for 0.6 mile to end (Memorial Boulevard).
- Right for 1.1 miles to Route 138A, which bears left. Here short ride bears left.
- Straight for 0.1 mile to Tuckerman Avenue. Bear right and immediately right again on Esplanade. Go 0.2 mile to first left. Go left for 100 yards to crossroads (Tuckerman Avenue).
- Right for one mile to stop sign (merge right). Purgatory Chasm on right just before stop sign.

- Bear right for 0.1 mile to fork at bottom of hill.
- Bear right for 0.4 mile to fork (Hanging Rock Road bears left).
- Bear left for 0.8 mile to crossroads (Third Beach Road).
- Straight for 1.9 miles to Old Mill Lane. Go left for 0.7 mile to end (Wapping Road).
- Left for one mile to where Third Beach Road turns left and Mitchells Lane bears right.
- Bear right for a half mile to Wyatt Road on left.
- Left for 1.1 miles to end. Merge left on Route 138 for 0.2 mile to Forest Avenue on right.
- Right for 0.9 mile to end (Route 114).
- Left for 0.3 mile to parking lot on right. (**Caution:** Route 114 is extremely busy. Safest to use sidewalk.)

Directions for the ride: 18 miles

- Follow first 14 directions of long ride, to junction of Memorial Boulevard and Route 138A.
- Bear left on Route 138A for 0.4 mile to fork.
- Bear left on Route 214 for 2.2 miles to end (Route 114), going straight at 2 traffic lights.
- Right for 0.2 mile to parking lot on left. (**Caution:** Route 114 is extremely busy. Safest to use sidewalk.)

Kennedy and Jacqueline had their wedding reception here, and later the estate was used as a summer White House.

A little farther along Ocean Drive is Brenton Point State Park, containing a magnificent stretch of coastline. You pass by Rosecliff, The Breakers, and Salve Regina College. The campus, perched on ocean-front cliffs and surrounded by mansions, is one of the most spectacularly situated in the country. Passing behind the mansions is the Cliff Walk, a footpath along the coast running from Memorial Boulevard to the promontory south of Bellevue Avenue. You can walk your bike along the northern half, but the path becomes progressively rougher south of Rosecliff.

Just beyond the mansion area, there is a downhill run to gently curving Easton Beach, a good spot for a swim. The road along the beach is a causeway, with the ocean on the right and Easton Pond on the left. Just ahead the short ride turns north, hugging the shore of the pond to return to the starting point.

The long ride heads farther east into Middletown, which provides a tranquil contrast to the bustle and opulence of Newport. You continue to follow the shore to Purgatory Chasm, a narrow cleft in the cliffs overlooking the ocean, and Second Beach. You bike past Saint Columba's Church, a graceful stone structure with a small cemetery beside it. After following the ocean for another mile, head inland back to the starting point, pedaling through broad expanses of open farmland.

In an area as historically and architecturally significant as Newport, it is impossible to put all points of interest on the route without turning it into a labyrinth. I have elected to follow the water, one of the city's most visually appealing features. The center of town and many historic landmarks are two or three blocks inland, and are best seen on foot.

33. Tiverton—Little Compton

Number of miles: 13 (25 with Little Compton extension, 32 with
    Westport-Adamsville extension)
Terrain: Gently rolling, with one long hill on the 32-mile ride.
Start: Stone Bridge Inn, Route 77, Tiverton. If parking is
    restricted, park where legal on Lawton Avenue, the side
    street next to the building.
Food: Country store and small restaurant in Little Compton.
    Gray's Ice Cream, corner of Routes 179 and 77, Tiverton.
    Country store and Abraham Manchester's Restaurant in
    Adamsville.

The southeastern corner of the state, spanning the slender strip of
land between the eastern shore of Narragansett Bay and the Massachusetts state line, is the best area of its size in Rhode Island for
cycling. The region is a pedaler's paradise of untraveled country
lanes winding past salt marshes, snug, cedar-shingled homes with
immaculately tended lawns, trim picket fences, and broad meadows sloping down to the bay. The center of Little Compton is the
finest traditional New England village in the state.

Tiverton, a gracious town hugging the shore of the mile-wide
Sakonnet River, is an attractive place to start the ride. Opposite the
starting point is a pier that originally was part of a stone bridge
over the river to Portsmouth. After the bridge collapsed during the
1938 hurricane, the Sakonnet Bridge, a mile to the north, was built
to replace it. Head south on Route 77, and after a short distance,
turn onto idyllic, narrow country lanes that hug the river. Neck
Road crosses a small inlet over a rustic, one-lane wooden bridge.
Two miles ahead go past a small, semicircular dam at the base of
Nonquit Pond. The short ride now returns on Route 77 to Tiverton.

The 25-mile ride follows Route 77 south, climbing onto a ridge
with dramatic views of broad meadows sloping down to the shore.
You pass Sakonnet Vineyards, Rhode Island's only commercial win-
ery, which is open to visitors every day except Sunday. After another few miles, you reach the center of Little Compton. The long
triangular green is framed by a handsome white church, an old-

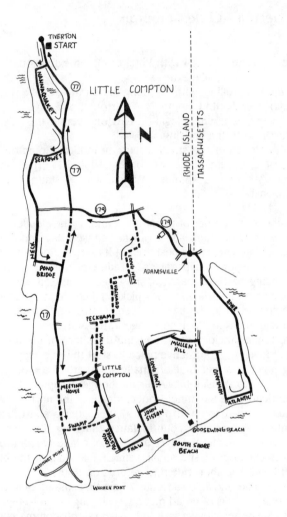

How to get there: From Route 195, exit south onto Route 24 in Fall River, and go about 5 miles to the Route 77 exit. Turn left at end of exit ramp and go one mile to parking lot on left.

Directions for the ride: 32 miles

- Left (south) out of parking lot on Route 77 for 0.7 mile to Nanna-quaket Road on right.
- Right across bridge for 1.6 mile to end. Merge right onto Route 77, go a half mile to Seapowet Road.
- Right for 2.2 miles to fork.
- Bear right on Neck Road for 1.3 miles to first left (Pond Bridge Road).
- Left for a half mile to end (Route 77). Here the 13-mile ride turns left.
- Right for 3.6 miles to Meeting House Lane (unmarked) on left, at traffic island (sign may say To the Commons). Here the 25-mile ride goes straight. Sakonnet Vineyards on left after about 1.5 miles.
- Left for 0.6 mile to fork, at Little Compton green.
- Bear left for 0.2 mile to end. Turn right for 1.2 miles to end (Swamp Road).
- Jog right and immediately left on Long Pasture Road. Go 0.6 mile to end (Shaw Road).
- Left for a half mile to end. (If you turn right at end for a half mile, you'll come to South Shore Beach).
- Left for a half mile to John Sisson Road. Right for 1.9 miles to fork where one branch bears right and the other branch goes straight. (At point where John Sisson Road turns 90 degrees left, a narrow lane on right leads 0.8 mile to Gossewing Beach.)
- Bear right for 0.9 mile to another fork at traffic island. Bear right on main road for 0.8 mile to end.
- Right for a half mile to Howland Road.
- Right for 1.1 miles to Atlantic Avenue, just before ocean.
- Left for 0.7 mile to end. (If you turn right at end, a dirt road leads a half mile to high boulder at tip of peninsula, with a great view).
- Left for 3.3 miles to stop sign (merge right). Bear right for half mile to end, in village of Adamsville.
- Left for 0.2 mile to fork. Bear right on Route 179 for 1.7 miles to end.
- Left (still Route 179) for 1.7 miles to traffic light (Route 77).
- Right for 4.5 miles to parking lot on right.

Directions for the ride: 25 miles

- Follow first 6 directions of long ride, to Meeting House Lane on left.
- Straight on Route 77 for 1.5 miles to Swamp Road on left. (If you go straight for about 2 miles, you'll come to Sakonnet Point, where the Sakonnet River meets the ocean.)
- Left for 1.3 miles to South of Commons Road.
- Left for 1.2 miles to center of Little Compton.
- Straight on Willow Avenue for 1.4 miles to end (Peckham Road).
- Right for 0.3 mile to Burchard Avenue. Left for 1.5 miles to end (Long Highway). Left for 1.6 miles to crossroads (Route 179).
- Left for 1.6 miles to traffic light (Route 77).
- Right for 4.5 miles to parking lot on right.

Directions for the ride: 13 miles

- Follow first 5 directions of 32-mile ride, to end of Pond Bridge Road (Route 77).
- Left for 5.8 miles to parking lot on right.

fashioned country store, and a weathered cemetery where Elizabeth Pabodie, daughter of John and Priscilla Alden and the first white girl born in New England, is buried.

The route heads north from the village along narrow lanes through a more wooded area. The Pachet Brook Reservoir is on your left; proceed north through forests and small farms to Route 179. This road leads down a long, gentle descent back to Route 77, where Gray's Ice Cream is on your left. It's good spot for a break before the last few miles of the ride. Along Route 77, within a few hundred yards of the intersection, is a historic district of gracious buildings, some recycled into crafts and antique shops. Finish the ride on Route 77, passing through broad meadows, and paralleling the Sakonnet River shore at the end.

The 32-mile ride heads toward the ocean in Westport, Massachusetts. Just before the state line, you can visit unspoiled South Shore Beach, a half-mile off the route, by turning right instead of left at the end of Shaw Road. Just ahead is Goosewing Beach, an even lovelier area at the end of an idyllic lane through broad pastures. In Westport, bike along the windswept coast, an unspoiled strand framed by salt ponds and cedar-shingled homes. At its eastern tip is the exclusive summer colony of Acoaxet. From here you have a relaxing run to Adamsville, 100 yards across the Rhode Island line in Little Compton, following the west branch of the Westport River. In the village are a country store in a rambling old wooden building, a monument to the Rhode Island Red breed of poultry, and Stone Bridge Dishes, makers of fine china. A long, steady climb out of Adamsville brings you to a stone church, built in 1841, on your left. Just ahead rejoin the 25-mile ride, just in time for the rewarding downhill run to Gray's Ice Cream.

The two longer rides can be extended by following Route 77 all the way to Sakonnet Point, the southernmost spot on the east side of the bay, with its nearly 360-degree panorama of ocean views. You can also visit Warren Point, just east of Sakonnet Point where gracious cedar-shingled homes keep watch above the rocky shoreline. To get there, go straight onto a small road where Route 77 curves sharply right, about a mile south of Swamp Road. It's about a mile to the point.

34. South County: Chariho Area

Number of miles: 16 (25 with East Beach loop)
Terrain: Rolling, with a tough hill on Woodville Road.
Start: Chariho High School, Hope Valley Road in Richmond, Rhode Island.
Food: Snack bar and grocery in Bradford. Snack bar and grocery at junction of Route 216 and I, for the long ride.

Just northeast of Westerly, almost at the southwest corner of Rhode Island, are the three small South County towns of Charlestown, Richmond, and Hopkinton, collectively called Chariho. The region abounds with winding rural roads that promise carefree cycling.

At the beginning of the ride there is the lovely village of Woodville, where three old, imposing houses stand opposite a fine little dam and millpond. A steady climb out of the village brings you onto a wooded ridge, where you turn south on Tomaquag Road, a twisting, narrow back road. The forest suddenly clears as you begin a glorious descent from the ridge, enjoying the sweeping view of the valley on your right.

Continue on into Charlestown, a thoroughly rural town except for some summer colonies along the splendid southern coast. In the past few years, Charlestown has become a leading center for competitive cycling in New England. Time trials, an event in which participants race a set distance (usually ten miles) against the clock rather than against each other, are held weekly on Route 1. With its wide shoulders and U-turn slots in the median strip, this highway is ideal for the event. Standard races are held weekly at Ninigret Park, on the runways of a former Naval Air Station. The park is two miles east of the route, off Route 1. Most of these events are open to novices. If you're interested, inquire at King's Cyclery in Westerly (596–6644) or at Stedman's Bike Shop in Wakefield (789–8664).

Buckeye Brook Road winds through wooded Burlingame State Park. You climb onto a ridge, and enjoy a fast descent with a fine view. Just before the end, you enter the tiny village of Wood River Junction.

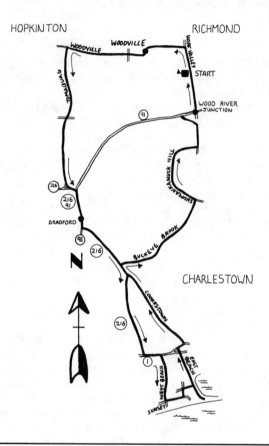

How to get there: From the north, exit west from Route 95 onto Route 138. Go 1.1 miles to traffic light where Route 3 goes straight and Route 138 turns right. Bear left at light and go four miles to school on the right. From the south, exit north from Route 95 onto Route 3, just past the state line. Go one mile to crossroads. Turn right at crossroads and go four miles to end. Turn right at end, and go 0.8 mile to school on right.

Directions for the ride: 25 miles

- Left out of parking lot for 0.8 mile to first left (Woodville Road).
- Left for 1.4 miles to crossroads. Continue straight for 1.4 miles to Tomaquag Road on left, just as you start to go down a hill.
- Left for 1.3 miles to crossroads (Ashaway-Alton Road). Continue straight for 2.1 miles to fork at bottom of hill.
- Left for 0.1 mile to end. Bear left on Route 216 for 0.3 mile to end (Route 91).
- Right for 0.9 mile to where Route 216 turns left and Route 91 goes straight.
- Left for 1.3 miles to Buckeye Brook Road on left (sign may say To North Camp). Here the short ride turns left.
- Straight for 0.3 mile to fork. Bear right on Route 216 for 2.2 miles to end (Route 1).
- Left (**Caution**) for 0.4 mile to West Beach Road on right (sign says Quonochontaug).
- Right for one mile to crossroads (Sunset Drive on right, Sea Breeze Avenue on left).
- Left for 0.4 mile to Midland Road on left (private road goes straight).
- Left for 0.2 mile to crossroads. Go right on main road for 0.2 mile to end (East Beach Road).
- Right for 0.3 mile to ocean.
- Make a U-turn at ocean and go 1.1 mile to Route 1.
- Cross Route 1 (**Caution:** Walk bike across median). Go 50 feet to end, at church.
- Right for 0.2 mile to first left (sign says Burlingame State Park).
- Left for 0.2 mile to park entrance road, which bears right.
- Straight on Klondike Road for 2.4 miles to end (merge right on Route 216).
- Bear right for 0.3 mile to Buckeye Brook Road on right (sign may say To North Camp). Right for 2.8 miles to end.
- Left on Shumankanuck Hill Road for 2 miles to end.
- Left for one mile to end (Route 91).
- Right for 0.3 mile to crossroads. Left on Hope Valley Road for 0.8 mile to school on left.

Directions for the ride: 15 miles

- Follow first 6 directions of long ride, to Buckeye Brook Road.
- Left for 2.8 miles to end (Shumankanuck Hill Road on left).
- Follow last 3 directions of long ride.

Instead of turning onto Buckeye Brook Road, the long ride continues south to the ocean along Quonochontaug Neck, a peninsula between two large salt ponds. Follow the paved road to East Beach, a fine example of the string of barrier beaches forming Rhode Island's southern shore. Beyond the road's end is the Ninigret Conservation Area, a narrow, unspoiled strip of land over three miles long that forms a frail barrier between the sea and Ninigret Pond. Heading north from the ocean, you pass the entrance to Burlingame State Park, a large expanse of woodland and swamp. The entrance road leads for about a mile to a campgrouund and a freshwater beach on Watchaug Pond. After winding through the woods for two miles on a narrow secondary road, turn onto Buckeye Brook Road to rejoin the short ride.

35. The Johnnycake Ride:
Kingston—Usquepaugh—Shannock

Number of miles: 17 (23 with Shannock extension)
Terrain: Gently rolling
Start: University of Rhode Island athletic area parking lot, Route 138, Kingston.
Food: Grocery on Route 138, West Kingston. Country store and soda fountain in Shannock.

The area just west of Kingston is delightful for bicycling, with dozens of traffic-free back roads weaving across the rural countryside. A highlight of this ride is the Kenyon Grist Mill in Usquepaugh, which grinds cornmeal into johnnycake flour using the same methods as when the mill was built in 1886.

The ride begins by heading through West Kingston, and following back roads along brilliantly green turf farms, white farmhouses, and stretches of woodland toward Usquepaugh. You pass Peter Pots Kilns, a manufacturer of fine ceramics and stoneware housed in an old mill and the Kenyon johnnycake mill. You are welcome to go in the mill and watch the cornmeal being ground between granite millstones. The johnnycake (a corruption of "journeycake") is a Rhode Island specialty introduced by the Narragansett Indians to the early settlers. A small shop across the road sells bags of the flour. The little pond and dam just beyond the mill provide the waterpower which still turns the millstones. The mill hosts an annual Johnnycake Festival near the end of October.

Just past Usquepaugh head south on Beaver River Road. This is the kind of lane you see photographed in country magazines, with ribbons of pastureland bordered by stone walls and rows of impressive shade trees. To your left, the small Beaver River ripples at the edge of the fields. A couple of miles ahead is the site of the Great Swamp Fight, which took place in 1675 during King Philip's War and resulted in the near annihilation of the Narragansett Indians. A monument commemorating the event stands off Route 2 on a dirt road. From here it's a short ride back to West Kingston along

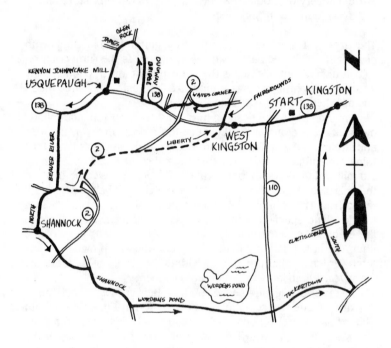

How to get there: Same as ride 24.

Directions for the ride: 23 miles

- Right out of parking lot on Route 138 for 0.7 mile to traffic light (Route 110 on left).
- Straight for 0.6 mile to crossroads immediately after railroad overpass (Fairgrounds Road).
- Right for 0.4 mile to crossroads (Waites Corner Road).
- Left for 0.8 mile to fork and bear left for 0.1 mile to Route 2.
- Straight for a half mile to end at Route 138. Bear right (don't turn 90 degrees right on Sand Turn Road). Go 1.1 mile to Dugway Bridge Road on right (sign may say Peter Pots Pottery).
- Right for 1.1 miles to fork immediately after small bridge.
- Bear left on Glen Rock Road for 0.4 mile to fork, and bear left again for 0.8 mile to Kenyon Grist Mill on left. Just ahead is a stop sign; bear right (almost straight) for 0.2 mile to end (merge right on Route 138).
- Bear right for 1.2 miles to Beaver River Road, just past small bridge. Go left for 2 miles to end. Here the short ride turns left.
- Right for 0.1 mile to fork.
- Bear left for 1.2 miles to end (village of Shannock).
- Left for 0.6 mile to crossroads (Route 2). To go to Shannock Spa, turn right for 200 yards instead of left.
- Cross Route 2 and go 0.7 mile to end (merge right).
- Bear right for 0.9 mile to Wordens Pond Road.
- Left for 2.9 miles to crossroads (Route 110). Continue straight on Tuckertown Road for 2.4 miles to end (Post Road).
- Left for 0.2 mile to South Road. Turn left for 1.6 miles to crossroads (Curtis Corner Road).
- Straight for 1.8 miles to end (Route 138) and go left for 0.8 mile to parking lot on right.

Directions for the ride: 17 miles

- Follow first 8 directions of long ride, to end of Beaver River Road.
- Left for 0.4 mile to wide fork with pine grove in middle.
- Left for 0.2 mile to end (merge into Route 2).
- Bear left for 1.8 miles to Liberty Lane. Bear right for 1.8 miles to Route 138.
- Right for 0.6 mile to traffic light (Route 110 on right).
- Straight for 0.7 mile to parking lot on left.

another narrow rustic road, with the University of Rhode Island just ahead.

The long ride heads a little farther south, following the Beaver River along another picture-book lane. Suddenly you round a bend and the antique mill village of Shannock lies before you. A cluster of gracious white homes with black shutters overlooks the Pawcatuck River, which flows over a unique horseshoe-shaped dam. Only a shell remains of the mill, a victim of fire. The Shannock Spa, an old-fashioned country store with a soda fountain, is a good spot for a breather.

A couple of miles beyond Shannock, a gentle downhill run brings you to the shore of Wordens Pond. After a relaxing ride along the water, head again through prosperous South County farms interspersed with forests. At the end, you'll finish with a flourish as you zip down Kingston Hill.

36. South Attleboro—Cumberland— Wrentham—North Attleboro

Number of miles: 17 (28 with Wrentham extension)

Terrain: Gently rolling, with one tough hill climbing up from the reservoir. The long ride is rolling.

Start: Washington Plaza, junction of Routes 1 and 123 in South Attleboro, Massachusetts.

Food: Grocery on Route 114 opposite Reservoir Road. Big Apple fruit stand and cider mill, Wrentham. Country store on corner of Route 121 and Hancock Street, Wrentham. Pizza at end.

The region straddling the Rhode Island-Massachusetts border is surprisingly rural considering that it's sandwiched between Pawtucket and North Attleboro. Its many quiet country roads are ideal for bicycling.

The ride begins in the suburban community of South Attleboro, just north of Pawtucket. The route angles northwestward into Cumberland, Rhode Island, on Mendon Road which turns into Abbott Run Valley Road. This long road is predominantly rural, but new homes keep springing up along it. You pass an open hillside which is now a housing tract, but around the next curve is open country again. This part of Cumberland, called the Arnold Mills section, is considered a desirable place to live.

When you reach Route 120, the village of Arnold Mills itself lies a half mile off the route to your right. It boasts a rickety old antique shop, a small dam, and an excellent Fourth of July parade. Continue north along the Diamond Hill Reservoir that provides Pawtucket's water supply. Parking was recently banned from this road, so you can pedal in peace without worrying about car doors opening in your face.

Just past the reservoir, the short ride crosses back into Massachusetts in North Attleboro. After a steep climb leading out of the watershed, the remainder of the ride is a delight—passing large, prosperous dairy farms. Then you come down from the ridge on a long, lazy descent. Near the end of the ride is the Abbott Run, a

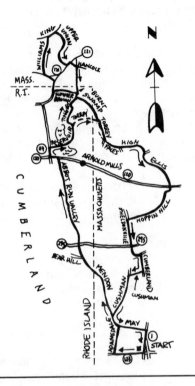

How to get there: From the south, exit north from I-95 onto Route 1A (the first exit in Massachusetts). Go one mile to Route 123 and turn left. The parking lot is just ahead on your right on the far side of Route 1. From the northeast, exit west from I-95 onto Route 123. The parking lot is two miles ahead on your right. From the west, exit south from Route 295 onto Route 1. Parking lot is two miles ahead on your right. By bike from Providence, head north on North Main Street. At Pawtucket line bear left on Route 122 (Main Street). Follow Route 122 for 4 miles to Route 123, then right for 3 miles to parking lot on left.

Directions for the ride: 28 miles

- Right out of south side of parking lot on Route 123 for 0.7 mile to Adamsdale Road. Right for 0.7 mile to end, at stop sign.
- Bear left on Mendon Road for 1.8 miles to fork (Bear Hill Road bears left). Bear right for 2.2 miles to end at Route 120.
- Left for 0.2 mile to traffic light (Route 114).
- Right for 0.6 mile to Reservoir Road.
- Right for 1.6 miles to fork (Torrey Road bears right, Tingley Road bears left). Here the short ride bears right.
- Bear left for 0.9 mile to fork (Burnt Swamp Road on right). Curve left on main road for 0.3 mile to Sumner Brown Road. **Caution:** Watch for bumps and gravel.
- Left for 1.6 miles to end (route 121).
- Right for 0.6 mile to one-way road; go left for 0.2 mile to end.
- Bear left for 0.2 mile to Williams Street.
- Right for 2.4 miles and bear right for 0.2 mile to Upper Union Street, just before Route 495.
- Right for 2.8 miles to end (Route 121).
- Left for 0.2 mile to Hancock Street.
- Right for 0.2 mile to diagonal crossroads (Burnt Swamp Road).
- Bear right for 1.3 miles to where Burnt Swamp Road turns left and main road curves right. Turn left for 0.8 mile to crossroads. **Caution:** Last quarter mile is bumpy.
- Left for 1.1 miles to second left (dirt road on right).
- Left for 0.4 mile to fork and bear slightly left for 0.7 mile to fork.
- Bear right on Ellis Road for 1.4 miles to crossroads (Route 120).
- Straight for 1.3 miles to end.
- Left for 1.1 miles to Cumberland Avenue on right, after Route 295 underpass.
- Right for 0.3 mile to first right (Cushman Road, unmarked); go right for 0.2 mile to end.
- Left (still Cushman Road) for one mile to end (Mendon Road).
- Left for 0.2 mile to fork; bear left on May Street for 0.7 mile to traffic light (Route 1).
- Right for 0.3 mile to parking lot on right.

Directions for the ride: 17 miles

- Follow first 6 directions of long ride to fork of Torrey Road and Tingley Road.
- Bear right on Torrey Road for 0.6 mile to crossroads.
- Straight for 1.1 miles to second left (dirt road on right).
- Follow last 8 directions of long ride.

stream flowing between two old stone embankments from the Diamond Hill Reservoir through Arnold Mills to the Blackstone River. Just before the parking lot is Fuller Memorial Hospital, a private psychiatric facility with a campuslike setting.

The long ride makes a loop through the rural, rolling countryside of Wrentham, Massachusetts. This is a gracious community on the outer fringe of the Boston metropolitan area, far enough from the city to be nearly undeveloped. The last mile of Williams Street crosses into Franklin, which in contrast to Wrentham is courting suburban growth. But soon you pedal past Wrentham's horse pastures and barns once again. Union Street ascends gradually onto a ridge with fine views; then you descend past the Big Apple, a large orchard featuring hot and cold cider, doughnuts, and freshly-picked apples in season. It's a refreshing rest stop on a nippy fall day. Just ahead you nick the northeast corner of Rhode Island on Burnt Swamp Road, passing small farms bordered by forest, before rejoining the short ride.

37. Seekonk-Rehoboth: Southern Ride

Number of miles: 16 (29 with southern extension)
Terrain: Gently rolling, with one hill. The long ride has an additional hill.
Start: K-Mart, junction of Routes 44 and 114A, Seekonk.
Food: Country store at corner of County and Reservoir Streets and at corner of Reed and Water Streets. Burger King and McDonald's on Route 44, one mile west of starting point.

The two towns of Seekonk and Rehoboth, just east of Providence across the Massachusetts state line, offer some of the finest cycling in the entire Rhode Island-nearby Massachusetts area. The region is fairly flat, unusually rural considering how close it is to the city, and protected by strict zoning laws that are preventing the onslaught of suburbanization. An extensive network of well-paved, narrow country lanes winds past large farms, a couple of ponds, and rustic, weathered old barns and farmhouses. The center of Rehoboth is a gem, with a perfect little dam and millpond, a fine small church, and the Goff Memorial building that holds the town library and hosts a classical music festival during the summer.

The proximity of the Seekonk-Rehoboth region to Providence makes it very easy to reach by bicycle, especially from the city's East Side. From the bridge at the end of Waterman Street that connects Providence and East Providence, it is only three or four miles to the start of this ride and the two following ones.

From Seekonk you bike past gentleman farms and large, gracious homes, and then cross into Rehoboth. Here you head to Rehoboth Village, the center of town, through a pastoral landscape of gently rolling farmland. The return run to Seekonk leads through more of this landscape. The long ride heads farther east and south through an even more rural area. You go along the Warren Upper Reservoir and follow the beautiful valley of the Palmer River, lined with large farms. Just ahead you pass Shad Factory Pond, a small millpond with a nice dam. From here you are a short ride back to the start.

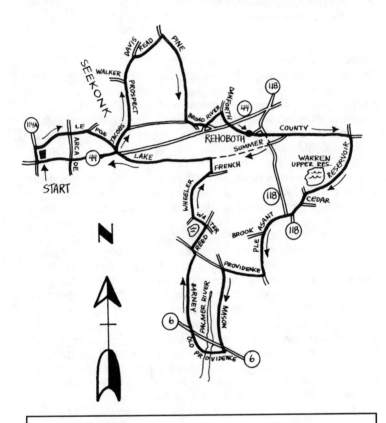

How to get there: From I-95, exit east onto Route 195 for about 2 miles to Taunton Avenue exit (Route 44). Follow Route 44 for about 2 miles to K-Mart on left, just past Route 114A. From the east, exit north from Route 195 onto Route 114A. Go 1.7 miles to Route 44. K-Mart is on far right corner. By bike from Providence, head east on Waterman Street, cross bridge, and take first exit. Just ahead road curves 90 degrees left onto Waterman Avenue. Go 0.6 mile to Route 44, at second traffic light, turn left and go 1.6 miles to K-Mart on left.

Directions for the ride: 29 miles

- Right out of parking lot on Route 114A (not Route 44) for a quarter mile to first right (Ledge Road).
- Right for 0.7 mile to crossroads (Arcade Avenue).
- Straight for 0.3 mile to fork. Bear right for 0.2 mile to another fork where Hope Street bears right. Straight (still Ledge Road) for 0.7 mile to end (merge right just before Route 44).
- Sharp left for 0.4 mile to Prospect Street.
- Left for 1.4 miles to fork and bear right (still Prospect Street) for a half mile to another fork. Curve right on main road for one mile to end (Pine Street).
- Right for 2.2 miles to end (Broad Street).
- Left for 0.3 mile to fork. Bear left on main road for 0.3 mile to another fork.
- Bear left down a little hill for 0.7 mile to end (Danforth Street).
- Right for 0.3 mile to crossroads (Route 44).
- Straight (**Caution**) for 0.8 mile to fork just past Rehoboth Village.
- Bear right on County Street for 0.3 mile to crossroads (Route 118). Here the short ride turns right.
- Straight on County Street for 2.2 miles to crossroads at top of hill.
- Right for 2 miles to end (Gorham Street).
- Left for 0.2 mile to end, merge right on Cedar Street for 0.6 mile to stop sign (Route 118).
- Turn right. Just ahead Route 118 turns right, but go straight for 0.7 mile to fork where Brook Street bears right and main road bears left.
- Bear left for one mile to Providence Street on right, just beyond fire station.
- Right for 1.3 miles to Mason Street, at traffic island.
- Sharp left for 1.9 miles to diagonal crossroads (Route 6), and go straight (**Caution**) for 0.1 mile to end (Old Providence Road).
- Right for one mile to diagonal crossroads (Route 6 again) and go straight (**Caution**) on Barney Avenue for 1.9 miles to end.
- Left for 0.1 mile to first right (Reed Street); right for 0.6 mile to crossroads and stop sign (Water Street).
- Left for 0.3 mile to fork at bottom of hill.

- Bear right for 1.1 miles to another fork (it's after Lake Street on right); bear left on Wheeler Street for 0.3 mile to end (Summer Street).
- Left for 0.3 mile to where main road curves left and Pond Street turns right. Curve left for 1.7 miles to end (merge left on Route 44).
- Bear left for one mile to traffic light (Arcade Avenue) and go straight for 0.7 mile to K-Mart on right.

Directions for the ride: 16 miles

- Follow first 11 directions of long ride, to Route 118.
- Right for 0.3 mile to crossroads.
- Right on Summer Street for 0.9 mile to fork. Bear slightly right (still Summer Street) for 0.6 mile to another fork.
- Bear slightly right again for 0.6 mile to where main road curves left and Pond Street turns right. Curve left for 1.7 miles to end (merge left on Route 44).
- Bear left for one mile to traffic light at Arcade Avenue and go straight for 0.7 mile to K-Mart.

38. Seekonk—Rehoboth
Northern Ride

Number of miles: 14 (26 with Rehoboth extension)
Terrain: Gently rolling, with two short hills.
Start: K-Mart, junction of Routes 44 and 114A, Seekonk, Massachusetts.
Food: Country store at corner of Fairview Avenue and Route 118. Country store at corner of County and Reservoir streets. Burger King and McDonald's on Route 44, one mile west of starting point.

The Seekonk-Rehoboth area is so ideal for bicycling, and so accessible to Providence (20 minutes by bike from the East Side), that it is worth including more than one ride through the two towns in the book. On this ride, we'll explore the countryside just north of the previous ride. The terrain is similar—pleasantly rolling with an occasional hill for variety—but the landscape is more wooded.

The ride starts from the Seekonk–East Providence line and heads north on Route 152, crossing the Turner Reservoir. After two miles, proceed onto a smaller road which leads into the more rural, eastern half of Seekonk. Here are the deep-green lawns of the Ledgemont Country Club, and just beyond it the Caratunk Audubon Sanctuary, an expanse of meadow, marshland, and forest crisscrossed by footpaths.

Just ahead turn east and then south on Pine Street, which climbs gradually through woodland, passing some new homes tastefully integrated with the landscape. At the top of the hill, just over the Rehoboth town line, are two radio towers a half mile apart. On the short ride, there's a gentle descent down the far side of the hill, first on Pine Street and then on a narrow lane with a few short steep pitches to give you a burst of speed. The route continues south across Route 44, the busy east-west road that slashes across the two towns on its way to Taunton. Heading west back into Seekonk, you go through a more open area with some large farms and two expanses of town-owned conservation land.

The long ride heads farther east along winding, wooded lanes

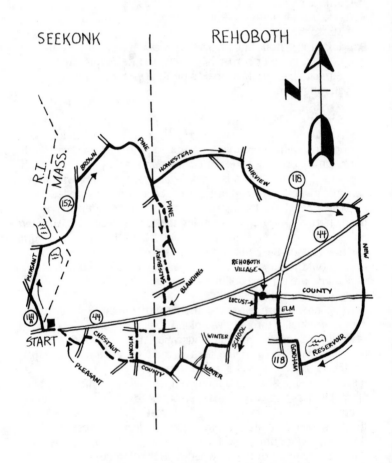

SEEKONK   REHOBOTH

N

R.I. / MASS.

PINE
BROWN
HOMESTEAD
FAIRVIEW
(118)
(152)
(114)
(44)
PINE
NEW
PLEASANT
(114)
SALISBURY
REHOBOTH VILLAGE
COUNTY
BLANDING
LOCUST
ELM
(114)
(44)
CHESTNUT
WINTER
SCHOOL
RESERVOIR
START
LINCOLN
COUNTY
WATER
(118)
GORHAM
PLEASANT

How to get there: Same as Ride 37.

Directions for the ride: 26 miles

- Right out of parking lot onto Route 114A for 0.6 mile to traffic light.
- Bear right immediately after light on Pleasant Street for 0.6 mile to wide crossroads (Route 152).
- Right for 2.1 miles to Brown Avenue; bear right for 1.3 miles to end (Pine Street).
- Right for 1.6 miles to Homestead Avenue on left. Here the short ride goes straight.
- Left for 1.4 miles to small crossroads. Go straight for a half mile to fork.
- Curve left on main road for 0.7 mile to end (Fairview Avenue).
- Right for a half mile to fork where main road curves slightly left again. Go left for 0.6 mile to crossroads (Route 118).
- Straight for 1.2 miles to fork at bottom of hill.
- Bear right for 0.3 mile to fork at top of hill.
- Bear right for 0.3 mile to traffic light (Route 44). Go straight for 1.8 miles to crossroads (County Street on right). Continue straight for 2.1 miles to end (Gorham Street).
- Right for 1.1 miles to crossroads (Route 118).
- Right for 0.8 mile to second crossroads (County Street). Left for a half mile to Locust Street, in Rehoboth Village. Left for a half mile to end.
- Right for 0.1 mile to fork. Bear left on School Street for 0.9 mile to Winter Street.
- Right for 1.1 miles to end. Then left for 0.2 mile to fork.
- Bear left for a quarter mile to crossroads (Water Street).
- Right for 0.3 mile to end, at bottom of hill.
- Left (still Water Street) for 0.4 mile to end, at large traffic island (County Street).
- Bear right for one mile to fork.
- Bear right on Chestnut Street for 1.5 miles to end (Arcade Avenue).
- Left for 0.1 mile to Pleasant Street; right for 0.4 mile to Route 44. Bear left (**Caution**) for 0.1 mile to K-Mart on right.

Directions for the ride: 14 miles

- Follow first 4 directions of long ride, to Homestead Avenue on left.
- Straight for 0.1 mile to fork.

- Bear left (still Pine Street) for 1.3 miles to narrow lane on right shortly after bottom of short, steep downgrade (Salisbury Street, unmarked).
- Right for one mile to end. Jog right and immediately left for 0.4 mile to crossroads (Route 44). Go straight (**Caution**) for 0.4 mile to end.
- Right for 0.6 mile to crossroads at top of hill (Lincoln Street).
- Left for 1.1 miles to crossroads (County Street).
- Right for 0.2 mile to fork (Chestnut Street bears right).
- Follow last 2 directions of long ride.

to Route 118, the main north-south road through Rehoboth. Beyond this road the countryside is even more rural. You pass a horse farm and descend to the unspoiled Warren Upper Reservoir. Just ahead is Rehoboth Village, a New England classic with a little dam and millpond, white church, and the handsome brick Goff Memorial building. The return trip brings you along delightful back roads through a harmonious mixture of forests and open fields, passing well-maintained farmhouses and grazing animals. You rejoin the short ride just after you cross the Seekonk line.

39. Seekonk—Rehoboth
One More Time

Number of miles: 21 (12 with shortcut)
Terrain: Gently rolling, with one short hill.
Start: D. J. Handlebars, 753 Fall River Avenue (Route 114A),
Seekonk, Massachusetts.
Food: None on the ride. McDonald's and Burger King on Route
114A, a half mile south of starting point.

The terrain and landscape of this ride through Seekonk and Rehoboth are similar to that of the other two rides, with little narrow roads winding past farms with weathered barns and stone walls.

The ride starts by heading east across Seekonk on County Street, which quickly leads you into the countryside. After two miles you cross the Rehoboth town line and turn south on Barney Avenue, an idyllic byway passing broad, prosperous farms along the Palmer River. Cross the river at the point where it begins to widen into a tidal estuary. On the far side is the Mason Barney School, a handsome, traditional brick schoolhouse. Proceed north along the opposite bank of the river, traversing more rich farmland full of cows and horses.

Along Chestnut Street the area becomes more wooded and you cross a low ridge with a good view on your left. Continue on to Route 118, the main north-south road through Rehoboth, which has a smooth surface, good shoulders, and not much traffic. Head north a short way and then turn west into the classic Rehoboth Village. Immediately after the gracious Goff Memorial, a lovely little dam appears on your left, followed by the traditional white church. On Locust Street is the Carpenter Museum, with exhibits of local history and rural artifacts.

Continue south through forests and small pastures on School Street, the kind of lane that seems to have been laid out with bicycling in mind. A couple of miles ahead, descend a gentle grade to the Shad Factory Dam, a picturesque spot for a rest or picnic lunch. The Palmer River begins here, flowing south for six or seven miles to Narragansett Bay. The remaining few miles of the ride bring you past a few more large farms and a residential area.

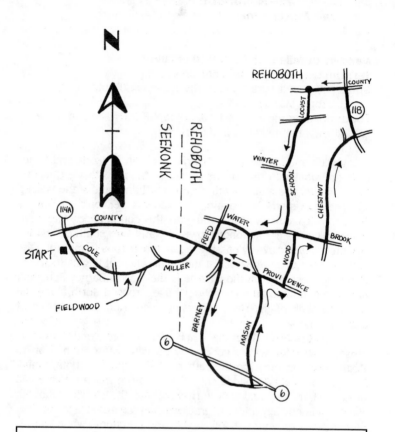

How to get there: Exit north from Route 195 onto Route 114A for 0.2 mile to bike shop on left, just past Showcase Cinema. By bike from Providence, head east on Waterman Street, cross bridge, and take first exit. Just ahead, road curves 90 degrees left onto Waterman Avenue. Go 0.6 mile to end, at second traffic light. Left for 1.8 miles to end, staying on Waterman Avenue. Left for 0.2 mile to traffic light (Route 114A). Right for a quarter mile to store on right.

Directions for the ride: 21 miles

- Left out of parking lot for 0.2 miles to traffic light.
- Right for 3.2 miles to Barney Avenue on right, just past Reed Street on left. Go right 0.1 mile to fork and straight (don't bear right on Wheaton Avenue) for 1.9 miles to Route 6.
- Cross Route 6 diagonally (**Caution** here). Go one mile to Mason Street, turn left for 0.1 mile to Route 6.
- Cross Route 6 diagonally (**Caution** again). Go 1.9 miles to diagonal crossroads at top of hill (Providence Street). Here the short ride bears left.
- Sharp right for 0.4 mile to Wood Street. Turn left for 0.8 mile to end (Brook Street).
- Right for 0.7 mile to crossroads at top of hill (Chestnut Street).
- Left for 1.7 miles to fork; bear right on main road for 0.1 mile to crossroads (Route 118).
- Left for 0.8 mile to second crossroads (County Street on right).
- Left for a half mile to Locust Street; turn left for a half mile to end.
- Right for 0.1 mile to fork. Bear left on School Street one mile to where main road curves left. Take it for 0.9 mile to end (Brook Street).
- Right for a half mile to fork.
- Bear right on Water Street for 0.6 mile to crossroads (Reed Street).
- Left for 0.6 mile to end (County Street).
- Right for 0.4 mile to first left (Miller Street); turn here for 0.9 mile to fork (Bradley Street bears right).
- Bear left for a half mile to fork (Fieldwood Avenue goes straight).
- Straight (don't bear left) for 0.4 mile to crossroads (Olney Street on right, Cole Street on left). Continue straight for 0.9 mile to Route 114A.
- Right for 0.1 mile to parking lot on left.

Directions for the ride: 12 miles

- Follow first 4 directions of long ride, to diagonal crossroads at top of hill.
- Bear left for 1.1 miles to second left (Miller Street). Turn here for 0.9 mile to fork.
- Follow last 3 directions of long ride.

40. Warwick Ride

Number of miles: 17
Terrain: Flat, with one gradual hill.
Start: Buttonwoods Plaza, corner of Route 117 (West Shore
Road) and Buttonwoods Avenue, Warwick.
Food: Numerous snack bars and grocery stores on West Shore
Road.

Warwick, located five to ten miles directly south of Providence, per-
sonifies the middle-class suburban community. When you hear the
name "Warwick," the first images that pop into your mind are probably places where you don't really want to bicycle—Interstate 95,
the airport, or dreary four-lane commercial arteries lined with car
dealers and shopping centers. But fortunately, Warwick has an extensive frontage along Narragansett Bay, with several peninsulas
and inlets piercing its shoreline. This ride explores that section of
Warwick.

At the beginning of the ride, head directly to the bay, where you
will follow the bike path around Warwick City Park. The park lies on
a wooded neck bounded by two small coves. The bicycle path,
which loops around the neck for about two and a half miles, hugging the water, is delightful.

Leaving the park, pedal through a middle-class residential area
and then head east on West Shore Road toward Oakland Beach, the
next peninsula. A small road heads down to the end, with Brush
Neck Cove on your right and modest homes on your left. When you
get to the tip of the peninsula, you can see for miles down the bay.
You return up the center of the peninsula and then head east to
Warwick Neck, the largest of the peninsulas on the ride. Loop
around Rocky Point, Rhode Island's only amusement park, located
directly on the bay. Treat yourself to a traditional Rhode Island seafood dinner in the cavernous Shore Dinner Hall here.

Just south of Rocky Point is Our Lady of Providence Seminary,
one of the most idyllic spots in the Providence metropolitan area.
On this large, graciously landscaped estate, a lane curves down a

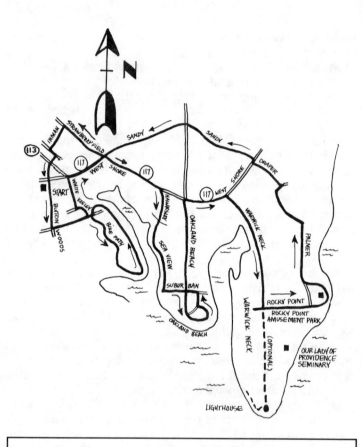

How to get there: Exit east from I-95 onto Route 117. Go a little over two miles to shopping center on right. By bike from Providence: Head south out of city on Elmwood Avenue to where Reservoir Avenue bears right. Continue straight for about 7 miles to Route 113 (Main Avenue). Left for one mile to Buttonwoods Avenue, which bears right at traffic light. Bear right for 0.3 mile to shopping center, just past traffic light.

Directions for the ride

- Right out of parking lot on Buttonwoods Avenue (not West Shore Road) for 0.3 mile to crossroads (Long Street on right, Asylum Road on left).
- Left for 0.4 mile to entrance to Warwick City Park straight ahead. Enter park, go 100 yards to bike path on right.
- Right for about 2.5 miles to end of path. (**Caution:** Watch for glass, leaves, debris, and pedestrians on path, and for shallow holes where posts used to be. Also watch out for traffic as you cross automobile roads.)
- Right for 50 yards to park exit, then straight for 50 yards to first right on Keeley Avenue. Go 0.1 mile to first right (White Avenue).
- Right for 0.4 mile to traffic light (West Shore Road, Route 117).
- Right for 1.1 miles to Hawksley Avenue on right, after Canfield Avenue.
- Right for 0.3 mile to crossroads and stop sign.
- Go straight on Sea View Drive and immediately bear right on main road. After 0.8 mile, road curves 90 degrees left on Suburban Parkway. Go 0.2 mile to wide crossroads (Oakland Beach Avenue).
- Right for 0.2 mile to beach parking lot. Loop counter-clockwise around lot to end.
- Right for 0.2 mile to divided crossroads (Suburban Parkway).
- Left for one short block to crossroads (Oakland Beach Avenue).
- Right for one mile to traffic light (West Shore Road).
- Right for 0.7 mile to Warwick Neck Avenue, after traffic light.
- Right for 1.1 miles to Rocky Point Avenue on left, at blinking light. To visit Our Lady of Providence Seminary, continue straight for 0.4 mile to entrance on left. Lighthouse is 0.8 mile beyond south entrance of seminary. Westford Avenue, on right just before lighthouse, follows the shore for a half mile, passing mansions.
- Left on Rocky Point Avenue for 0.4 mile to park entrance.
- Straight into park. Follow main road for 2 miles to Draper Avenue on left, at stop sign.
- Left for a half mile to end (West Shore Road).
- Jog right and immediately left on Sandy Lane. (**Caution**). Go 0.9 mile to traffic light (Warwick Avenue).
- Straight for 1.1 miles to traffic light (Strawberry Field Road).

- Right for 0.6 mile to Inman Avenue (house number 332 on corner).
- Left for 0.3 mile to end (Parkway Drive).
- Jog left and immediately right (still Inman Avenue) for 0.4 mile to shopping center on right, just past second traffic light.

broad grassy hillside to the bay, and then climbs to the tall stone tower that forms the focal point of the estate. If you wish, you can continue south for about a mile to the tip of the peninsula, where a Coast Guard lighthouse guards the bay. From here you have to backtrack to Our Lady of Providence and the road to Rocky Point. The return leg to the starting point heads inland through middle-class residential neighborhoods.

41. Swansea—Somerset—Dighton—Rehoboth

Number of miles: 17 (30 with Rehoboth extension)
Terrain: Gently rolling, with one moderate hill and one tough
     one.
Start: McDonald's, Route 6, Swansea.
Food: Grocery in Dighton. McDonald's at end.

This ride takes you through the gently rolling countryside along the west bank of the lower Taunton River, the major river in the southeastern part of Massachusetts. The route parallels the river for several miles and then returns along the ridge rising just inland from the west bank. The long ride heads farther west into farm country, and then finishes with a relaxing run along Mount Hope Bay, the broad estuary at the mouth of the river.

Start from Swansea, a pleasant rural community midway between Providence and Fall River, and just far enough from either to have so far avoided suburban development. The center of town boasts a handsome stone town hall with a clock tower, built in 1890, and a fine stone library next door.

From Swansea you traverse a low ridge into Somerset, lying along the Taunton River across from Fall River. Most of Somerset is suburban, but you bike through the older and less-developed northern portion of town. Follow the river on a narrow street lined with fascinating old buildings in a wide variety of architectual styles, and then continue to the center of Dighton, another attractive riverfront town extending westward into gently rolling farm country.

From Dighton the short ride heads back toward Swansea along a ridge with impressive views of the river and the surrounding landscape. The longer ride heads farther inland to Rehoboth, a beautiful rural town of farms and winding, wooded roads. Cross briefly into a little strip of Rhode Island to the shore of Mount Hope Bay, just back over the Massachusetts line. After a scenic, curving run along the shore, it's a short ride back to the start.

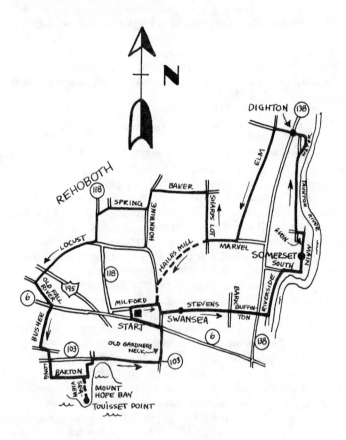

How to get there: From Route 195, exit east on Route 6 and go a half mile to McDonald's on left. By bike from Providence: Head east on Waterman Street, cross bridge, and take first exit. Just ahead, road curves 90 degrees left onto Waterman Avenue. Go 0.6 mile to end, at second traffic light. Left for 1.8 miles to end, staying on Waterman Avenue. Left for 0.2 mile to traffic light (Route 114A). Right for 1.1 miles to Route 6. Bear left for about 7 miles to McDonald's on left.

Directions for the ride: 30 miles

- Turn right out of *back* of parking lot onto Milford Road for 0.6 mile to end. Go right for 0.2 mile to first left, at traffic light. **Caution:** Speed bumps when you leave parking lot.
- Left for 2.8 miles to traffic light at bottom of hill (County Street, Route 138).
- Straight for 0.3 mile to end, at Taunton River.
- Left for 0.4 mile to fork, and bear right on main road for 1.1 miles to diagonal crossroads where South Street bears right.
- Follow South Street for 0.4 mile to end (Main Street).
- Left for a half mile to Avon Street (last left before end); go left for 100 yards to end, at traffic island.
- Right for 2.6 miles to Water Street, a little lane on right just after small concrete bridge.
- Right for 0.6 mile to Route 138, at blinking light; go straight for 0.4 mile to crossroads (Elm Street). Left for 3 miles to end (Marvel Street on right).
- Right for one mile to crossroads (Sharps Lot Road). Here the short ride goes straight.
- Right for 1.7 miles to crossroads. Turn left on Baker Road for 1.6 miles to end (one-room schoolhouse at intersection).
- Left for a half mile to Spring Street. Right for one mile to fork.
- Bear left on main road for 0.2 mile to end (Route 118).
- Left for 0.8 mile to end (water tower on right).
- Right on Locust Street for 1.8 miles to end (Old Fall River Road).
- Left for 0.8 mile to end. Bear left on Route 6 and immediately turn right on Bushee Road (**Caution** here). Go 1.4 miles to end (Schoolhouse Road).
- Left for 0.2 mile to Long Lane. Right for 0.2 mile to crossroads (Route 103)
- Straight for 2.6 miles to crossroads and blinking light (Route 103 again), staying on main road. (You can turn right at the bay onto Seaview Avenue; it runs along the water for 1 mile to dead end.)
- Right for 1.3 miles to blinking light at top of hill (Old Gardners Neck Road). Left for 0.9 mile to traffic light (Route 6). **Caution** turning left.
- Left for 0.9 mile to McDonald's on right.

Directions for the ride: 17 miles

- Follow first 9 directions of long ride, to junction of Marvel Street and Sharps Lot Road.
- Straight for 1.8 miles to end (merge left at stop sign).
- Bear left for a half mile to Milford Road on right.
- Right for 0.6 mile to back entrance of parking lot on left.

42. Border Patrol: Exeter—Voluntown, Connecticut—Sterling, Connecticut—Greene—Escoheag

Number of miles: 33 (sorry, no short ride)
Terrain: Hilly.
Road surface: 2.4 miles of dirt road.
Start: Beach Pond parking lot, Route 165, Exeter, just before Connecticut border. On beach days you can avoid the parking fee by starting at the picnic area 0.1 mile east, at top of hill.
Food: Pizza at Plainfield-Sterling line. Snack bar and grocery in Sterling. Snack bar at Stepping Stone Ranch, Escoheag.

The western three miles of the state that hug the Connecticut border come as close to true wilderness as you'll find in Rhode Island. The first half of the ride heads north along the Connecticut side of the state line, climbing onto ridges with spectacular views and plunging into small valleys. The second half returns south along the Rhode Island side, passing through deep boulder-strewn forests with an occasional house or farm. You'll pass Step Stone Falls, a little-known beauty spot tucked away on a dirt road, where a stream cascades over a succession of broad, step-like rocks.

The ride starts from Beach Pond, a good-sized pond straddling the state line. You immediately cross into Voluntown, Connecticut, a small village surrounded by miles of woods and farmland. Its main claim to fame is that for some reason the Committee for Nonviolent Action, one of the first organizations opposed to the Vietnam War, was located here. You wind up and down on narrow roads passing small farms, and then head north on Route 49, a paradise for bicycling. There's a very gradual climb onto Ekonk Hill, a high open ridge where hundreds of cows graze contentedly. From both sides of the road, superb views sweep to the horizon. At the highest point the spindly silhouette of a fire tower, set back from the road, rises skyward. You are now in Sterling, a slender town midway between the northeast and southeast corners of Connecticut.

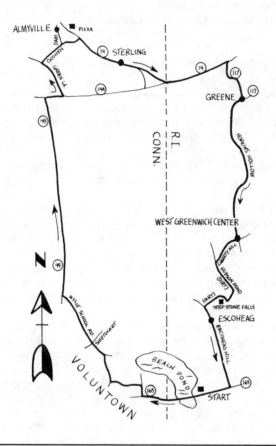

How to get there: From the north, head south on I-95 to exit 6 (Route 3). Turn left (south) at end of ramp for about 6 miles to Route 165 on right. Turn right for about 8 miles to Beach Pond. From the south, head north on I-95 to exit 4 (Route 3). Go north on Route 3 for about 3½ miles to Route 165 on left. Turn left on Route 165 for about 8 miles to Beach Pond.

Directions for the ride

- Right out of parking lot for 1.3 miles to Bennett Road on right, at top of gradual hill.

- Jog right and immediately left for a half mile to end (merge left at stop sign).

- Sharp right for 0.3 mile to Wylie School Road, at bottom of hill.

- Left for 1.2 miles to crossroads (Shetucket Pike), and continue straight for 1.4 miles to crossroads (Route 49). Notice former one-room schoolhouse on corner.

- Right for 5.7 miles to end (Route 14A). Go right for 0.2 mile to Green Lane.

- Left for 1.5 miles to Goshen Road (first right).

- Right for 0.8 mile to unmarked road (first left).

- Left for 0.1 mile to blocked-off bridge; notice dam on right. Backtrack to main road; left for 0.3 mile to end (Route 14). For pizza or groceries, left on Route 14 for 0.1 mile.

- Right on Route 14 for 5.9 miles to Route 117 on right, staying on main road.

- Right for 1.7 miles to end (Route 117 turns left).

- Turn right. After 2.2 miles, main road curves sharply left up steep hill. Continue 2.1 miles to crossroads.

- Right on Liberty Hill Road for 0.9 mile to end (Hudson Pond Road), at bottom of hill.

- Left on dirt road. (**Caution:** Get the feel of the road first. If it's soft, it's safest to walk because it is easy to skid and fall.) After 1.1 miles, main road curves 90 degrees right. Just ahead is a small bridge. Continue a half mile to another small bridge. (Step Stone Falls on left). Continue 0.6 mile up steep hill to end (Escoheag Hill Road). Do yourself a favor and walk the bumpy and rocky hill.

- Left for 2.3 miles to crossroads (Route 165).

- Right for 1.6 miles to parking lot on right.

Route 49 brings you into the tiny village of Sterling Hill, which has a lovely white church. Drop off the ridge in a screaming descent which keeps getting steeper and steeper. In the valley lies the mill village of Almyville, with two old mills and a lovely terraced dam on the Moosup River. From here it's a couple of miles to the center of Sterling, a small mill town with a row of identical houses facing the millpond. Only the shell remains of a large brick mill, destroyed by fire a few years ago. On the other side of the road, in a triumph of folk art, someone has painted a waving American flag on a large rock on the shore of the pond.

Two miles beyond Sterling cross back into Rhode Island, where the land immediately becomes more wooded, and arrive in the picturesque village of Greene (part of Coventry), with its rambling wooden houses, old church, and tiny library. From here a winding lane leads past unspoiled Tillinghast Pond to West Greenwich Center. It sounds metropolitan, but the only thing here is a crossroads and the little West Greenwich Baptist Church, dating from 1750.

Another fast downhill brings you to a dirt road. The first mile is flat and usually hard-packed, going alongside Kelley Brook. Step Stone Falls (sometimes called Stepping Stone Falls) is a short distance ahead on your left, at the second bridge. From the falls, the road twists up a very steep, rutted hill which you'll want to walk. At the top is paved road again which goes through the village of Escoheag. This community boasts a fire tower, a few houses, two tiny cemeteries, an equally tiny church, and the town hot spot, the Stepping Stone Ranch. This sprawling establishment is primarily a place to board and ride horses, with innumerable trails webbing through the surrounding state forest lands. On summer weekends, the enterprising owner hosts special events like the popular Cajun Festival on Labor Day weekend (it is the largest outside of Louisiana).

Just past the Ranch cross the town line into Exeter and enjoy the downhill run to Route 165. From here it's two miles back to Beach Pond and a well-earned swim.

43. The Northern Border Ride:
Slatersville—Uxbridge—Millville
Mendon—Blackstone

Number of miles: 11 (26 with Massachusetts loop)
Terrain: Rolling, with several short hills.
Start: Slatersville Plaza, junction of Routes 5, 102, and 146A in
   North Smithfield, Rhode Island, near the Massachusetts line.
Food: Lowell's, Route 16, Mendon (26-mile ride). Excellent ice
   cream and fish & chips. There's a pizza place and bakery
   serving coffee in the shopping center at the end.

The region just west and northwest of Woonsocket, straddling the
center of Rhode Island's northern border, is ideal for bicycling. Here
is the rural New England of Currier-and-Ives prints, with narrow
wooded lanes meandering alongside stone walls, cozy log cabins
nestled amid pine groves, and unspoiled small towns. The long ride
passes within a quarter mile of the Southwick Wild Animal Farm, a
large collection of animals from all over the world.

   The ride starts a half mile south of the Massachusetts border
and immediately passes through the lovely mill village of Slatersville. The triangular green is framed by a traditional, white New
England church and gracious homes dating from around 1810. Just
ahead is the dignified town hall with tall white pillars. Across the
road, a complex of Victorian stone and brick mills lies in the steep
valley of the Branch River.

   A mile out of town is an impressive two-tiered dam on your
left. Head west, just below the state line, along untravelled back
roads that bob up and down short wooded hills. The route turns
north on Ironmine Road, which crosses the state line into Uxbridge,
Massachusetts. Turn east, following more narrow country lanes just
north of the Rhode Island border. It's mostly downhill to the valley
of Blackstone River, where you cross Route 146. Just ahead parallel
the river and arrive in Millville, a mill town that has seen better
days. Just after you turn away from the river on the short ride
toward Rhode Island, you pass a handsome stone church standing
proudly above the town. From here, it's a mile back to the starting
point.

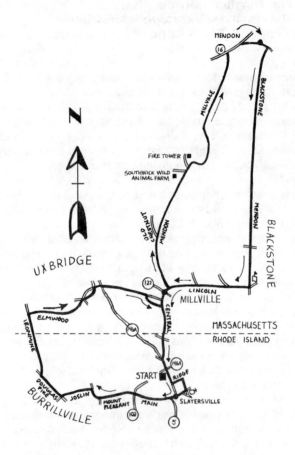

How to get there: From the south, take the Slatersville-Forestdale exit from Route 146. Turn right at the end of the exit ramp, then immediately left at end, and go one mile to parking lot on left. From the north, head south on Route 146 to Route 146A on right. Turn right on 146A and go a mile and a half to parking lot on right, just past the traffic light.

Directions for the ride: 26 miles

- Right out of parking lot on Route 5 (not Route 102 or 146A) for 0.4 mile to Ridge Road. Go left for 0.1 mile to end.
- Right for one block to crossroads (church straight ahead).
- Right for 1.2 miles to crossroads (Route 102). Continue straight for 0.9 mile to third left (Joslin Road, unmarked).
- Left for 0.8 mile to crossroads (Douglas Pike).
- Right for 0.8 mile to Ironmine Road, and bear right for 1.8 miles to Elmwood Street on right.
- Right for 1.6 miles to five-way intersection (Chestnut Street on left). Straight for 0.3 mile to crossroads and stop sign.
- Right for 0.1 mile to crossroads (Route 146A).
- Straight for one mile to fork; bear right on smaller road for 0.4 mile to end (Central Street, in Millville). Here the short ride turns right.
- Left for 0.3 mile to traffic light (Route 122). (**Caution:** Wire-grate bridge at bottom of hill becomes very slippery. If road is wet walk your bike.)
- Straight across Route 122, and turn immediately left on Chestnut Hill Road. Go 1.8 miles to fork.
- Bear right on main road for 4.4 miles to end (merge right on Route 16). Southwick Wild Animal Farm on left after 0.8 mile (on Vineyard Street); fire tower on left after one mile.
- Bear right for 0.2 mile to fork where a smaller road bears right downhill (sign says to Bellingham).
- Bear right for 0.4 mile to Blackstone Street on right, while going downhill.
- Right for 5.5 miles, staying on main road, to second crossroads (Lincoln Street). School on left corner.
- Right for 0.9 mile to fork. Bear slightly left downhill for 0.9 mile to crossroads (Route 122). Straight for 1.5 miles to end (merge left on Route 146A).
- Bear left on Route 146A for 0.2 mile to shopping center on right, just past traffic light.

Directions for the ride: 11 miles

- Follow first 8 directions of long ride.
- Right for 1.2 miles to end (merge left on Route 146A).
- Bear left for 0.2 mile to parking lot on right, just past traffic light.

The long ride heads farther north into Massachusetts, making a loop which begins and ends in Millville. A mile out of town, you pass the Chestnut Hill Meeting House, a simple, white wooden church built in 1769. After another mile, Vineyard Street is on your left. Here the ride continues straight ahead, but you may turn left for a quarter mile to visit Southwick Wild Animal Farm. Just 0.2 mile beyond Vineyard Street, there is a narrow lane on your left which goes uphill. If you turn onto the lane for 0.2 mile and then turn right onto a dirt road for 100 yards you come to an unfenced fire tower. The view from the top is breathtaking, and Boston's skyscrapers, 35 miles to the northeast, are just barely discernible on a very clear day.

When you come to Route 16, you have a fine view to your right from the top of a ridge before you reach the hilltop town of Mendon. When you leave Route 16, the parking lot for Lowell's Restaurant will be on your left. This is a great rest stop, with superb ice cream and fish and chips. Just beyond is a graceful white church and the old town hall. Leaving Mendon, ascend a small ridge with a superb view on your left, and then enjoy a long, lazy downhill run back into Millville, where you rejoin the short ride for the brief stretch back across the Rhode Island border to Slatersville.

44. Putnam—Woodstock—Thompson, Connecticut

Number of miles: 16 (34 with Woodstock extension)
Terrain: Rolling, with a tough hill near the end. The 34-mile ride is hilly.
Start: Pulaski Park, off Pulaski Road in West Glocester, at Connecticut line.
Food: Grocery at corner of Routes 21 and 44. Snack bar on Route 169, Woodstock (long ride). Country store at crossroads near end of ride.

On this ride, you'll explore the inspiringly beautiful ridge-and-valley country in the northeastern corner of Connecticut just west of the Rhode Island border. The long ride goes through some of the finest scenery in the book. The rolling terrain is somewhat challenging, but the panoramic views from the hilltops and some exhilarating downhill runs will more than reward your efforts. Here is rural New England at its best—rambling old farmhouses, weathered red barns with woodpiles nearly stacked beside them, and stone walls zigzagging across sloping fields filled with grazing cows and horses.

Pulaski State Park, a large expanse of woodland on the Connecticut border, is a good place to begin the ride. Just after you leave the park, you cross into Connecticut, heading west on small hillside lanes with fine views of the neighboring ridges. After several miles, the short ride heads north to the handsome town of Thompson, a traditional New England village with a white church, a stone library, and the elegant Vernon Stiles Inn clustered around the green. Two miles out of town off the route is the Thompson Speedway, one of New England's leading automobile racetracks.

Shortly after you leave Thompson, you ascend onto a ridge with a spectacular view, and zip down the far side to the Quaddick Reservoir, which straddles both sides of the narrow road. From here, it's two miles up and down a steep wooded hill back to Pulaski Park and a swim in the pond.

The long ride continues into Connecticut, first reaching Putnam, an old mill town with an impressive dam across the Quine-

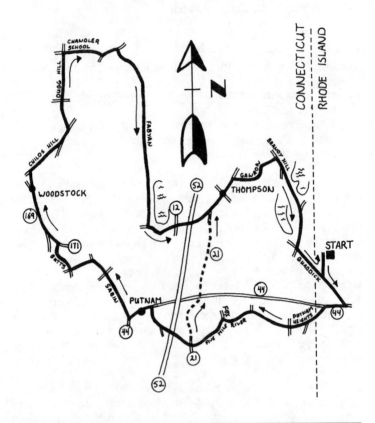

How to get there: From the east, head west on Route 44 until you come to Route 94 on your left. Continue on Route 44 for another mile to Pulaski Road on your right. Turn right on Pulaski Road and go one mile to park. There are three parking lots about a quarter of a mile along the park access road. The third lot adjoins a small pond with a beach. From the west, go east on Route 44 to Rhode Island border, then take your first left onto Pulaski Road.

Directions for the ride: 34 miles

- At end of park entrance road, straight on Pulaski Road for 0.8 mile to end (Route 44).
- Right for 0.3 mile to Putnam Heights Road; bear left for 1.7 miles to crossroads (East Putnam Road).
- Straight for 1.1 miles to fork (Tucker Hill Road bears right).
- Bear left for 0.7 mile to fork; curve left on main road for 1.1 miles to crossroads (Route 21). Here the short ride turns right.
- Straight for 1.6 miles to stop sign. Straight on Route 12 for 0.9 mile to end (Route 44).
- Left for 0.6 mile to Sabin Street (unmarked) on right, immediately after small bridge. Route 44 curves left at intersection.
- Right for 1.4 miles to crossroads; then straight for 0.2 mile to fork.
- Bear left for a half mile to crossroads. Go right for 1.1 miles to end (Route 171).
- Left for 1.5 miles to where main road curves left and small road goes straight, at top of hill, in Woodstock.
- Straight for 1.5 miles to end. Bear left for 0.3 mile to fork.
- Bear left on Dugg Hill Road for 2.7 miles to second crossroads (Chandler School Road). It comes up suddenly while you're going downhill.
- Right for 1.2 miles to end. Merge left at bottom of hill for 0.2 mile to Fabyan Road on right. Take it for 5.3 miles to end.
- Left for 1.3 miles to traffic light (Route 12).
- Straight for 1.7 miles to crossroads at top of hill, in Thompson.
- Straight for 0.4 mile to Gawron Road.
- Right for 1.4 miles to end (Brandy Hill Road).
- Right for 0.3 mile to where O'Leary Road bears right and main road goes straight downhill. Go straight for 1.8 miles to end.
- Bear right for 0.6 mile to crossroads.
- Left for 1.5 miles to park entrance on left (sharp left).

Directions for the ride: 16 miles

- Follow first 4 directions of long ride, to Route 21.
- Right for 1.8 miles to crossroads (Route 44).
- Straight for 1.9 miles to end (merge right on Route 193).
- Bear right for 0.4 mile to crossroads, in Thompson.
- Follow last 5 directions of long ride.

baug River. From Putnam it's several miles to the unspoiled hilltop town of Woodstock, a classic New England jewel. Framing the large green are a stately white church, the handsome main building of Woodstock· Academy, and the Bowen House. This ornate, pink Gothic mansion (also called Roseland Cottage) was built in 1846 by Henry C. Bowen, a businessman who entertained several Presidents there at Fourth of July gatherings during the 1880s and 1890s. Before you leave Woodstock, ride 100 feet down a service road behind one of Woodstock Academy's buildings for a superb view of the area.

You'll exult in the sustained mile-long descent out of Woodstock. At the bottom turn north on Dugg Hill Road, a lane that climbs up to a ridge with inspiring views of the rolling countryside. A few miles farther on, ride along the top of West Thompson Dam, high above its lake, before climbing out of the valley to Thompson, where you rejoin the short ride.

Acknowledgments

Some of the photographs were supplied by the Rhode Island Department of Economic Development. Mr. Ted Metcalf gave me access to the photo collection and helped to choose photos that could best capture the various landscapes of the state. Mr. George E. Lambert at the Rhode Island Department of Environmental Management provided me with helpful histories and descriptions of state parks.

Many of the rides were originally mapped out in whole or in part by the following members of the Narragansett Bay Wheelmen, to whom I extend my thanks:

> Ted Ellis—Rides 1, 18
> Ray Young—Ride 5
> Tom Bowater—Rides 6, 9, 21, 24
> Warren Hinterland—Rides 14, 27
> Tom Boyden—Ride 16
> Ken Becket—Ride 20
> Jack McCue—Rides 28, 38
> Bob Vasconcellos—Ride 29
> Bob Corwin—Ride 32
> Ed Ames—Rides 33, 37
> Earl St. Pierre—Ride 36
> Matt Rosenberg—Ride 40
> Phil Maker—Ride 41
> John Lanik—Ride 43

Many of the improvements and modifications to the rides in the first and second editions were suggested by Jack Fahey. Leesa Mann helped me verify many of the rides for accuracy.

Enoy all the books in Globe Pequot's "Short Bike Rides" series:

Short Bike Rides on Cape Cod, Nantucket & the Vineyard
Short Bike Rides in Connecticut
Short Bike Rides in Greater Boston and Central Massachusetts
Short Bike Rides on Long Island
Short Bike Rides in New Jersey
Short Bike Rides in Rhode Island

Also enjoy Globe Pequot's "Short Walks" series:

Short Nature Walks on Cape Cod & the Vineyard
Sixyt Selected Short Nature Walks in Connecticut
Short Nature Walks on Long Island

Availabe at your bookstore or direct from the publisher. For a free catalogue or to place an order, call 1-800-243-0495 (in Connecticut, call 1-800-962-0973) or write to The Globe Pequot Press, Box Q, Chester, CT 06412.